grow your own fruit & veg in

plot, pots or growbags

the A-Z guide to
growing and cooking farm-fresh food

Steve Ott, Emma Rawlings
& Roxanne Warwick

foulsham

The Oriel, Thames Valley Court, 18
SL1 4AA, England

Foulsham books can be found in all good bo

ISBN: 978-0-572-03494-8

Copyright © 2008 Mortons Media Group Lt

Photographs by Pam DesChamps, John Wilk

Published in association with *Kitchen Garden* magazine (previously published as
Homegrown) by Mortons Media Group Ltd, Media Centre, Morton Way, Horncastle,
Lincolnshire LN9 6JR. Tel 01507 523456

Cover photograph © James Murphy

A CIP record for this book is available from the British Library

The moral right of the authors has been asserted

Steve Ott has worked in commercial horticulture all his life, growing everything from
pot plants to parsnips in his garden in Lincolnshire. He is the editor of *Kitchen Garden*,
Britain's best-selling monthly magazine dedicated to allotment gardeners.

Emma Rawlings is a professional horticulturalist and gardening writer. A keen
grower of fruit and vegetables, Emma has tended several allotments, as well as
keeping a vegetable plot in her garden at home in Rutland. She is deputy editor of
Kitchen Garden.

Roxanne Warwick has a passion for good, local and ethically produced food, which
has led her to recipe research and development. She tutors at Betty's Cookery School
in Harrogate and is the cookery expert for *Kitchen Garden*.

Printed in Dubai

Contents

Contents

Introduction	5
Preparing to grow	7

How to grow your own vegetables | 9

Artichokes	10
Asparagus	11
Aubergines	13
Beetroot	14
Broad beans	16
Broccoli	18
Brussels sprouts	20
Cabbages	22
Cauliflowers	24
Carrots	26
Celeriac	28
Celery	29
Chicory	30
Courgettes	31
Cucumbers	33
Endive	35
French beans	37
Garlic	39
Kale	41
Kohlrabi	43
Leeks	44
Lettuces	47
Onions & shallots	49
Parsnips	52
Peas	55
Peppers	57
Potatoes	59
Radishes	62
Runner beans	63
Salad leaves	65
Spinach	68
Squashes	69
Sweetcorn	72
Swiss chard	74
Tomatoes	75
Turnips	78

How to grow your own herbs | 79

Basil	80
Bay	81
Chives	82
Coriander	83
Dill	84
Fennel	85
Marjoram	86
Mint	87
Parsley	88
Rosemary	89
Sage	90
Tarragon	91
Thyme	92

How to grow your own fruit | 93

Apples	94
Apricots	97
Blackberries	98
Blueberries	101
Cherries	103
Currants	105
Figs	107
Gooseberries	109
Grapes	111
Peaches	113
Pears	115
Plums	117
Raspberries	119
Rhubarb	121
Strawberries	122
Useful terms	125
Index	127

Introduction

The easy-to-follow A-to-Z format of this practical guide takes you through the crops commonly grown in the UK and explains the essential tasks you will need for success both in the garden and in the kitchen.

Everyone loves to eat healthy food, and more and more people are discovering the benefits of growing their own fresh produce. No wonder – home-grown produce has so many advantages over shop-bought food: it tastes better, is guaranteed free from harmful pesticides and, since it hasn't travelled half way around the world to reach your plate, is environmentally friendly, too. It's also fun, great exercise and can bring the family together.

Gone are the days when owning an allotment was seen as the preserve of men. More women than ever before are taking up their trowels – indeed it is common to see whole families enjoying life on the allotment with many sites having long waiting lists for vacant plots.

Some would-be growers are put off by believing that growing your own takes lots of knowledge or a great deal of space. This is a shame since it is so easy and satisfying to do and can be done on the smallest plot.

A complete guide to growing and cooking your own fruit and veg, this superb practical guide shows just how easy it can be by providing you with all the information you need – whether you are a beginner or experienced grower. The A-to-Z format is easy to follow and looks at the most popular crops, explaining all the essential tasks you will need for a bumper harvest, whether you have an allotment, a vegetable plot in the garden, or simply a few tubs or a growbag on the patio or a balcony.

This guide takes the muck and mystery out of growing vegetables, fruit and herbs by showing exactly when and how to sow, how to tend, and how to harvest, prepare and store the most popular varieties. It will give beginners the confidence they need to grow their own five-a-day for their families. And, of course, there is a mouthwatering, easy-to-follow recipe or meal idea for every fruit and vegetable to inspire you, no matter how basic your cooking skills.

Preparing to grow

You don't need an allotment or a big garden to grow vegetables or fruit. Large pots or growbags will do. If you have a tiny garden, then devote a sunny part of it to growing a few vegetables. It can be as small as a square metre! If you don't have space, just grow some attractive and tasty vegetables in the flower border, or plant some vegetables in containers on the patio.

If you want to mix in a few vegetables with your flowers, you could sow a line of mixed salad leaves at the front of a border: not only will they spice up your salads but they will look attractive, too. You could try training some runner beans, or an apple, plum or pear tree, up a sunny wall or fence. For the tiniest spaces, plant a tumbler-type cherry tomato in a hanging basket, along with a couple of bedding plants. Strawberries are also ideal for a hanging basket or a large tub. You'll find many more ideas for small spaces in this book.

BADLY NEGLECTED PLOT

If you are lucky enough to acquire an allotment, the plot will probably be covered in weeds, or even woody brambles if it has been badly neglected.

You don't need to cultivate it all in the first year. Take your time and concentrate on a small area first so it doesn't become overwhelming – or risk damaging your back! Sow and tend this area well and by the end of your first growing season you will still have a few crops. Meanwhile, you can deal with the rest of the plot to prepare it and make it easier to clear when you do start to work on it. You can start to dig that over in the autumn and begin to sow from the following spring.

If you cover the weeds with some black permeable membrane, which is sold by the metre at garden centres, you can leave the remaining plot untended for up to a year. Spread the membrane over the ground, making sure it is fixed well at the edges by digging them into the soil or placing bricks around all sides. This will smother the weeds and make the clearing process much easier.

Brambles and saplings need to be cut down with shears or a strimmer. If the plot is large, use a strimmer first to cut all the top growth back to ground level, then dig this area over well, removing as many of the roots as you can.

If you want to use all the ground for growing as quickly as possible, then either dig over the whole area, removing all the weed growth, or to make the job easier, apply the systemic weedkiller glyphosate. The chemicals travel right through the plant and kill the roots. It will take several weeks to have an effect but suddenly the weeds will turn yellow and die. At this stage you can rake off the dead material and dig over the plot.

NEW PLOT FROM A LAWN

In order to turn a piece of lawn into a vegetable plot, you have two choices:

Remove the turf: If you have a good, deep soil, then removing the turf is a good option as you will get very little regrowth of grass. For large areas, you can hire equipment to strip off the turf. For small areas, it is easy to do by hand by pushing a spade under the turf about 5cm/2in below the surface. It can literally be lifted up in long strips. And the discarded turf need not be wasted: just stack it up in a big pile grass-side down. This will ensure the grass does not grow but in a few months you will have a beautiful stack of good quality soil that can be put back on your vegetable plot.

The soil should be dug over at least a spade's depth but preferably a bit deeper to loosen up the compacted layers. With soil that is very heavy clay or very sandy, it would be beneficial to incorporate plenty of farmyard manure or garden compost before sowing or planting.

Spray the grass with weedkiller: This is the easier option and particularly good if you have poor or thin soil. The first 2.5cm/1in below the surface of grass is usually good quality, so ideally you want to keep it; stripping off the turf will remove some of it.

Many weedkillers can be used, but if you spray with glyphosate, this will get right to the grass roots and kill any perennial weeds in the turf. It is best applied on a bright, but not hot, day and, although it takes two to three weeks to show results, you only have to wait a day or two after spraying before digging in the turf.

This can be a tricky job, as the grass may be quite compacted and it is hard to break up the clods of grass and roots. It is best to dig a 30cm/12in deep trench first, and then turn the turf back into this. The aim is to bury the grass clumps so that you have an easier soil surface to cultivate. Sowing can begin as long as there is no regrowth. Should the grass start to come through, it will require another spray before planting.

THE BEST TIME TO START

Sowing vegetables: Between March and September.

Planting fruit: Container-grown trees can be planted any time as long as they are kept well watered, but the best time is between September and April.

Trees bought by mail order from specialist mail order suppliers are usually supplied as bare-rooted (freshly dug from the nursery). They are sent out from late autumn to early spring.

Raspberries and other cane fruit are best planted in the dormant season from autumn to early spring. Strawberries can be planted from March up until late spring and again in autumn.

SUNNY BORDER

A sunny area of flower border will make an excellent vegetable plot, as most vegetables and fruit do better in the sun. You can either dig up and remove what plants are in the border and start afresh with vegetables, or plant a few vegetables among the flowers.

CONTAINER GROWING

A lot of fruit and vegetables can be grown in containers and you'll find the information on the right size of pot to use and how to go about it in the sections on individual crops.

The key to growing produce in containers is to use a large enough pot and to keep the compost continually moist. The best compost to use is a John Innes No. 2 or 3, which contains loam. This is heavier than a peat or peat-free compost so the pots will be more stable. Also it will not dry out as quickly as the peaty or bark-based composts and is easier to rewet if it does dry out.

SOWING YOUR SEEDS

Sowing in pots: The more tender vegetables are best sown in pots, cell trays or seed trays first; small seedlings then need to be pricked out to give them plenty of room. Plant out seedlings when there is no danger of frosts – at the end of May or beginning of June. When sowing, use a John Innes seed compost or a good multi-purpose compost.

Suitable crops: Crops that prefer to germinate in pots include tomatoes, peppers, aubergines, sweetcorn, French beans and squashes. Other crops are sometimes started off in pots because they are more vulnerable to pests if sown directly in the ground. These include brassicas (cauliflower, cabbage), broad beans, lettuce and leeks.

Preparing to sow outdoors: The soil needs to be dug over and then raked until the surface is broken down to a fine tilth – a level surface made up of fine crumbs of soil. This well-prepared surface is necessary for tiny seed sowing but not so vital if planting seed potatoes or onion sets.

Planting: Use a line to make a straight row. You don't need to sow in straight lines but it enables you to recognise the seedlings when they appear.

Make a narrow groove or seed drill with a stick or corner of a hoe. Water the seed drill, as it helps to settle and soften the bottom of the drill and ensures the seed will be surrounded by moisture.

Sow the seeds, sprinkling them sparingly along the drill if they are tiny, then cover with fine soil, crumbling it through your fingers if necessary. Avoid covering the seeds with large solid clods of earth or stones.

Water the ground again using a fine rose on a watering can and wait for germination.

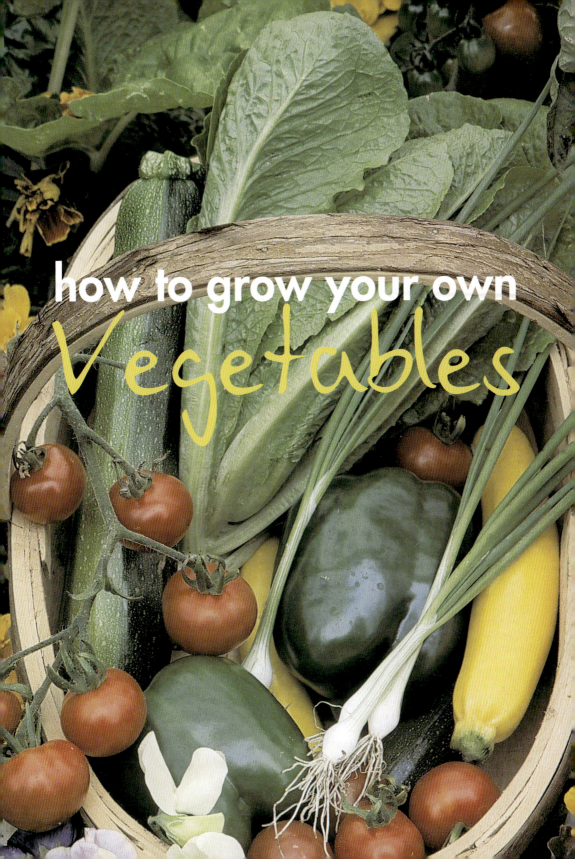

how to grow your own
Vegetables

Artichokes

Jerusalem and Chinese artichokes are grown for their tuberous knobbly roots, globe for its flower buds. Here, we focus on the globe artichoke, which is easy to grow. It forms a large silver-grey, thistle-like plant up to about 1.2m/4ft high and wide, so it requires plenty of space. In winter, the decorative leaves die back to re-emerge in spring.

Varieties

'Green Globe Improved': Makes a large plant up to 1.8m/6ft in height. Produces many good quality buds for harvesting.

'Violetta Di Chioggia': A stunning plant that is ideal for the flower border or large tub. Silvery-grey foliage is topped by dark purple flower buds instead of the usual green.

Growing tips

Sowing and planting

Artichokes like a light soil in a sunny spot. If your soil is clay, consider growing a plant in a large pot.

Globe artichokes can be grown from seed sown directly into the ground in April. However, they won't produce flowers until the following year at the earliest and will be vulnerable in

In the kitchen

Globe artichokes make a delicious starter with a warm, buttery vinaigrette. They are best cut and eaten fresh.

Preparation and cooking: Rinse and remove the darker outer leaves, and trim off the stalk and thorny leaf tips. Slice off the top to leave a tight bulb.

Cook whole for a good 20 minutes or more, depending on the size, either in boiling water to cover, or wrapped in foil and baked in the oven at 200°C/400°F/gas 6/fan oven 180°C, both with a squeeze of lemon juice. They are ready to eat when the bracts (bud leaves) pull away easily. Tear off each bract one by one and dip the base in a sharp dressing until you get to the hairy fibrous 'choke'; cut this away with a sharp knife and eat the remaining fleshy heart.

♥ *High in fibre, vitamin C, iron, potassium, calcium and phosphorus.*

their first winter. Ideally, buy young plants that will have been propagated from root offsets. If you know someone with a large clump, ask if you can have a root or two, which can be taken from the side of the plant, preferably with a shoot attached. Plant about 90cm/3ft apart and keep well watered.

Apply a generous helping of garden compost, bark or farmyard manure around the plants in May to help conserve soil moisture and keep weed growth down.

Growing on

In the first year, cut off any flower buds that form to allow the plant to conserve its energy for bulking up the crown. In the second year, you can begin harvesting.

The first bud to be produced is often a main 'king' bud and should be removed. Subsequent smaller buds will form, which when they have reached the size of a tennis ball are ideal for eating.

Calendar

- Plant in tub of John Innes No. 3 compost and split plant after 3–4 years.
- In the garden, plant Apr–May and harvest during the summer from year two.

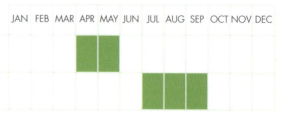

	JAN	FEB	MAR	APR	MAY	JUN	JUL	AUG	SEP	OCT	NOV	DEC
Sowing/ planting time				■	■							
Harvest time							■	■	■			

Growing tips

Sowing and planting

Asparagus is a long-term crop so it pays to get the site in order well before planting. This means removing as much of the perennial weeds as possible. Asparagus likes a well-drained, sunny site, enriched with farmyard manure or garden compost.

The crowns are usually bought in the dormant season and planted in early spring. Place them in a trench about 30cm/12in wide and 20cm/8in deep, and splay the spidery roots out over a slight ridge along the bottom. Cover with about 5cm/2in of soil and firm down.

Growing on

Some spears will appear in the first year but resist cutting these as you want them to grow into feathery, fern-like stems and develop strength in the crown. The stems will put on lots of good growth during the summer and then you can take a small harvest in the following spring, gradually increasing the amount you take each year as the plants become established.

Keep the beds weed-free but avoid hoeing in early spring as you will cut off the spears.

Start harvesting at around May time and continue until early to mid June, to allow the shoots to develop and grow into the feathery stems. If you don't let these grow, the crowns will weaken and fewer shoots will form the following spring.

As the stems are quite spindly, they may benefit from being supported with string around the outside to keep the plant growing straight

Asparagus grows from spidery roots that act as storage organs in winter, when the plant dies back. In early spring, the first young shoots that appear are the asparagus spears that we so love. Some of these are harvested, then the remaining ones are allowed to grow into ferny stems. Asparagus is easy to grow and relatively pest-free.

Varieties

'Cito F1': An excellent hybrid from France that produces heavy crops.
'Connover's Colossal': A good early-cropping variety that is also available as a seed.
'Franklim': A popular variety producing a heavy crop of thick spears.
'Gijnlim': A good variety that has outperformed others in growing trials. The spears appear from mid to late April and, being an all-male variety, it does not produce seeds, so there are no self-sown seedlings to weed out.
'Jersey Knight Improved': An all-male hybrid producing thick, tasty spears.

Fact file

- A bed of asparagus can last between eight and 20 years.
- When cutting, use a sharp knife and cut about 8cm/3in below soil level.
- Plant some crowns of early and later varieties to extend the harvest period.

In the kitchen

This delicious shoot loses its sweetness rapidly, so eat it fresh soon after cutting. Old asparagus can taste woody and dull.

Preparation and cooking: To prolong storage time, plunge into boiling water for a few seconds, then refresh in ice-cold water. Wrap in a damp cloth and keep cool, then reheat as required.

Keep cooking simple; asparagus should be the star off the show. Boil or steam for 5–10 minutes, then drain and serve with plenty of butter; or chargrill the spears on a griddle or barbecue. Egg or white sauces make perfect accompaniments. Enjoy tender stems raw or al dente with mayonnaise or hollandaise.

Storage and freezing: Asparagus doesn't keep for long, just two or three days in a fridge. It can be frozen but it requires blanching first. Sort out thick stems from thin and blanch the thick ones for four minutes and the thin ones for two. Roll in kitchen paper to remove excess water, then freeze in a plastic box.

♥ *A single helping of asparagus (about 150g/3oz) can provide nearly twice the daily recommended amounts of vitamins B6, C and E.*

ASPARAGUS TART

You can serve this straight from the oven or leave to cool and serve with salad. It also freezes well.

Serves 4–5

about 20 asparagus spears
3 large eggs
150ml/5fl oz double cream
90ml/3fl oz full-cream milk
½ tsp ground coriander
salt to taste
225g/8oz shortcrust pastry
20cm/8in diameter baking tin, not less than 4cm/1½in deep, greased

1 Preheat the oven to 180°C/350°F/gas 4/ fan oven 160°C.
2 Stack the asparagus upright in a pan and steam for 5–10 minutes until tender. Cut into 5cm/2in pieces, discarding any tough stems.
3 In a bowl, whisk the eggs lightly. Gradually whisk in the cream, milk, coriander and salt.
4 Line the tin with the pastry. Place the asparagus on top, and pour over the filling.
5 Bake in the oven for about 45 minutes until lightly browned.

and upright. In autumn the foliage will start to yellow, so remove it by cutting the stems at the base, leaving 3cm/1in stumps above ground. In late winter, apply a little fertiliser, such as Growmore, and spread some compost.

Container growing

Growing asparagus in a pot is not usual as the crowns need to have plenty of room and

enough water and nutrients to keep the plant strong. However, it can be done. Choose a large container 90cm/3ft square to house one good crown. Mulch each year with some horse manure for a taster of fresh-cut spears – although you won't gather a feast!

Calendar

- Plant crowns in Apr.
- Sow seeds 2.5cm/1in deep in a prepared seed bed in Apr, then prick out. Plant out next spring.
- Harvest spears from established plants May–mid Jun.

	JAN	FEB	MAR	APR	MAY	JUN	JUL	AUG	SEP	OCT	NOV	DEC
Sowing/planting time				▉								
Harvest time				▉	▉	▉						

Aubergines

The aubergine is becoming a popular crop to grow as our taste for exotic fruit and vegetables expands. The aubergine plant is attractive, forming a lovely bushy shrub with prettily shaped, downy leaves. It needs a long, relatively hot summer to produce a decent crop of fruits, so be sure to plant your aubergines in a sunny spot.

Varieties

'Baby Rosanna': Perfect compact plant for the patio. Produces small golf-ball sized black fruits throughout the summer.
'Calliope': A new variety that produces pretty purple-pink fruits streaked with cream. Plants are spineless.
'Mohican': Produces long slender white fruits.
'Moneymaker': A classic dark purple fruited aubergine.

Growing tips

Sowing and planting
Use small 9cm/3½in pots or cell trays, filled with multi-purpose compost. Firm the soil gently and sow about eight seeds on the surface of each pot before covering with a sprinkling of compost. In cell trays put one seed per cell. Water well and place in a propagator or on a warm windowsill. They require a temperature of around 20°C/68°F to germinate. As soon as the seedlings emerge put in a light spot on a windowsill.

Growing on
Move seedlings into their own individual pots of multi-purpose compost as soon as they are large enough to handle. Water well and put back on a warm light windowsill. When the plants are about 30cm/12in high, remove the growing

In the kitchen
The aubergine originated in the East and many of its culinary uses reflect this. It is best eaten when young and shiny.
Preparation and cooking: Earlier varieties always had to have the cut surfaces rubbed with salt to draw out the bitter juices, but today's varieties do not need this treatment. However, rubbing in some salt will prevent them from absorbing too much of the cooking oil or juices.
They can be used in a variety of dishes from the classic Greek moussaka to roasting thick slices in a hot oven with chunks of pepper, onion, garlic and courgette generously drizzled with olive oil.
♥ *Antioxidants, vitamin A, potassium.*

tip to encourage other shoots to grow.
If placing aubergines outside, wait until June when all danger of frost has passed. Keep the compost moist but not too wet. Once the flowers form, feed with tomato fertiliser.

Container growing
Aubergines can be grown in a large pot on a sunny patio. Standard-sized varieties will need a pot 30cm/12in in diameter, while compact plants can grow in smaller ones.

Fact file
- The aubergine produces pretty mauve flowers.
- When the flowers appear, give the plant a mist of water to encourage the blooms to set.
- Pick fruits while they are still young and shiny.

Calendar
- Sow Feb–Mar.
- Plant in pots or growbags Apr–May under cover.
- Place outside on patio in the container in Jun.
- Harvest Jul–Sep.

	JAN	FEB	MAR	APR	MAY	JUN	JUL	AUG	SEP	OCT	NOV	DEC
Sowing/ planting time		☂	☂									
Harvest time							▓	▓	▓			

Beetroot

produces heavy yields. Most varieties (right) are ideal for the maincrop or mid-season sowings.

LONG BEETROOT

'Cheltenham Green Top': A popular long-rooted variety that needs a good deep soil that is not stony and is free-draining. Ideal for sandy soils.

Beetroot is unique in its colour and flavour. It is more popular in Eastern Europe and the USA, where it is used more in hot dishes. In the UK it is often pickled as well as used in salads. The best beetroot is definitely home grown because you can lift small roots when they are at their tastiest and most tender.

Varieties

Beetroot come in different shapes and colours – the most popular are the red, round varieties or globe. These don't require such a good, deep soil as the long-rooted types, and mature quicker. Always choose a bolt resistant variety if sowing early as the cooler weather may encourage premature flowering.

CYLINDRICAL BEETROOT

'Cylindra': An oval-shaped beetroot that is excellent for winter storage.

GLOBE VARIETIES

'Albino': A white globe variety that does not 'bleed' if the flesh is cut. It does not store as well as the reds.

'Boltardy': A very popular red beetroot ideal for early sowings as not prone to bolting.

'Burpees Golden': An orange variety with yellow flesh. It is a mild and tender variety and some say it has a superior taste to the red types. The young leaves can be steamed or added to salad.

'Detroit 2': Another popular variety that

Growing tips

Sowing and planting

Sow beetroot seeds in shallow seed drills about 2.5cm/1in deep and about 10cm/4in apart. If two or more seedlings appear at each sowing station, remove the excess seedlings to leave one. Leave about 30cm/12in between rows to allow room for growth.

Ideally sow short rows of beetroot every month to get a succession of roots to harvest.

Growing on

As the seedlings grow keep the ground moist and weed free. If the ground is allowed to dry out and then suddenly becomes wet it can cause the roots to split. Also periods of drought may lead to bolting. When the roots are about golf-ball size or a little larger, they can be harvested. Remove alternate roots to allow the remaining ones to grow on.

Fact file

- Roots that are lifted in autumn can be placed in layers in boxes of sand or dry compost and stored in a shed or garage.
- Beetroot seeds are actually a fruit and each cluster contains several seeds. However, there are some varieties that are monogerm, meaning they contain only one seed. Using these prevents the need for thinning later on.
- Germination can take up to two weeks.

In the kitchen

Beetroot is not just a salad ingredient but is also ideal for wine-making and soups, with its distinctive sweet, earthy taste. It can be a year-round vegetable, eaten fresh from June until September, then stored or pickled until about March. Through the season you can enjoy the young tender leaves, similar to spinach, and robust stalks, braised, as well as the globular root.

When lifting fresh beetroot, it is best to cut off the leaves leaving a short stump, as cutting into the flesh will cause it to 'bleed'.

Preparation and cooking: Prepare the roots by washing gently in cold water; do not remove the root at the base or cut into the top to remove the stump of stalk. Leave these intact and boil for one to two hours depending on the size. On removing from the pan, simply rub off the skins, remove the tops and thin root and serve hot or allow to cool. Beetroot is best cooked slowly, to enhance the sweetness, and combined with a little acidity to lift the flavour – a squeeze of citrus juice over a raw beetroot salad or a touch of cider vinegar in soups.

Beetroot juice will stain all it touches. Either use gloves or rub your hands with lemon juice to remove stains.

♥ *The dense colour means it is high in flavonoids – strong antioxidants, which can help prevent cancers. Good source of folate, the natural form of folic acid. High in vitamins A, C, K and calcium.*

Container growing

There is no reason why beetroot should not be grown in a container as long as you can keep the compost moist. With this in mind, a larger container, at least 38cm/15in diameter, is best as it won't dry out too often. Beetroot can be sown closer together in a container at about 5cm/2in apart and the result will be numerous smaller roots. Use John Innes No. 3 compost and place the container in a sunny spot.

BEETROOT MUFFINS

Makes 12

200g/7oz plain flour
25g/1oz cocoa
1 tbsp baking powder
100g/4oz sugar
50g/2oz butter, softened
1 tsp vanilla essence
2 eggs, beaten
120ml/4fl oz milk
100g/4oz raw beetroot, grated
100g/4oz chocolate drops

1 Preheat the oven to 180°C/350°F/gas 4/ fan oven 160°C. Grease or put paper cases in muffin tins.
2 Mix together the dry ingredients.
3 Stir in the remaining ingredients until just blended.
4 Spoon into the tins and bake for about 20 minutes until just firm.

Calendar

● For very early crops, sow Mar under cloches.
● Sow Apr, then another row in May for succession.
● Sow early Jun to provide roots for winter storage in moist sand.

	JAN	FEB	MAR	APR	MAY	JUN	JUL	AUG	SEP	OCT	NOV	DEC
Sowing/ planting time			🌱	■	■	■						
Harvest time						■	■	■	■	■		

Broad beans

A great crop for sowing in autumn, or late winter, for some delicious beans when there is little else in the garden. These large, leafy plants produce big pods that contain either white or green beans for cooking. The tips of the plants can also be picked and eaten, so can the whole small pods.

Varieties

'Aquadulce Claudia': Grows to 1m/3ft so may need some support. Best variety for early or late sowings. White seeds.

'Bunyard's Exhibition': A white-seeded variety that grows up to 1.2m/4ft so needs some support, too. It is an old variety that has remained popular because it produces good crops in all sorts of soil.

'Crimson-flowered': An unnamed heritage variety growing to about 1m/3ft. Superb flowers and beans.

'Imperial Green Longpod': Another tall one at 1.2m/4ft with green seeds. As its name suggests, it produces long pods with up to nine beans in each.

'The Sutton': A short variety growing to about 30cm/12in high with white seeds. A good choice if you don't have a lot of room.

Growing tips

Sowing and planting

Broad bean seeds are large, making them easy to sow, and they are traditionally sown in a double row about 20cm/8in apart, often in a zig-zag line. Scoop out a shallow trench about the width of a spade and about 3–5cm/1–2in deep in which to plant your beans.

The double row of plants will give you a greater harvest from a smaller area. Cover the seeds with soil and water well. It will take seven to ten days for the seedlings to emerge.

Growing on

Keep the plants well watered in dry weather, especially once they flower and start to produce pods.

Some broad bean varieties grow quite tall and once they start to produce pods become top heavy. So give them some support by placing four stakes at the corners of the crop and tying string around them.

As soon as some pods have started to form,

Fact file

- Grow the crimson-flowered broad bean, a heritage variety, in your flower borders for its pretty two-tone red flowers.
- It takes about 14 weeks between sowing and harvesting the first beans.
- Broad beans are not just good to eat, they also do wonders for the soil. When the plants have finished cropping, cut off the tops but leave the roots in the ground. These have nodules that fix nitrogen from the air.

nip off the tops of the plants. This tip takes a lot of the plant's energy, which you want to redirect into growing the pods. It will also take away the part of the plant that attracts the dreaded blackfly, a problem with broad beans.

You can harvest the pods when they are 5–8cm/2–3in long. These can be cooked and eaten whole. Alternatively, wait until they are more than 13cm/5in long and have filled out. Split open a pod to see if the beans are large enough to harvest. The smallest beans are the tastiest.

SAVORY BEAN SALAD

This recipe can be used as a side dish or as a starter, served warm with some crusty bread.

Serves 2–4

100g/4oz young broad beans, podded
1 tbsp chopped savory
3 tbsp olive oil
juice of 1 large lemon
sea salt
freshly ground black pepper
1 avocado

1 Lightly steam the beans until tender with the chopped savory.
2 Mix the oil with lemon juice, salt and pepper and add to the beans.
3 Halve the avocado, remove the skin and stone, slice the flesh and add to the beans.
4 Turn the salad until everything is coated with the dressing and serve.

In the kitchen

Broad beans are best eaten when small, fresh from the pod.

Preparation and cooking: Toss lightly boiled or steamed, young beans in vinaigrette or into salads, or team with garlic, butter and fresh mint leaves. You can eat the small pods whole, prepared like runner beans, sliced and lightly boiled. The growing tips can be eaten too. Older beans should have individual outer shells removed. Break open with your nail and pop the beans out. Plunge into boiling water for a few minutes until tender. Don't be tempted to add salt as it will toughen the skins. Turn them into a delicious seasonal mash by boiling until soft, then blend to a purée and serve with lamb.

Storage and freezing: Don't keep fresh beans too long. To freeze, remove the beans from the pods, wash well and blanch for three minutes in boiling water, then cool, pack in boxes and freeze. They will keep for about 12 months.
♥ *High in fibre, protein, vitamins A and C.*

Container growing

Broad beans can be grown in a pot as long as it is at least 60cm/2ft in diameter and depth to provide enough space for up to six plants. A potful of crimson-flowered beans will look pretty but for a good reliable harvest try growing the dwarf variety 'The Sutton'.

Use a John Innes No. 2 or 3 compost because this will hold moisture better than a peat or coir-based one. Do not let the pot dry out, especially when the pods are forming.

Calendar

● Sow under cover early Feb, then into the ground Mar–May.
● Sow 'Aquadulce Claudia' Nov in milder areas on free-draining soil to harvest May.
● Cover with a cloche in winter.

	JAN	FEB	MAR	APR	MAY	JUN	JUL	AUG	SEP	OCT	NOV	DEC
Sowing/ planting time		☁	■	■	■						■	
Harvest time						■	■	■	■	■		

Broccoli

Broccoli is a highly nutritious vegetable. You will really notice the difference in flavour with your own broccoli and, being so fresh, it will contain even more vitamins and health-giving properties. It belongs to the brassica family and there are three types: white and purple sprouting broccoli, and calabrese.

Varieties

CALABRESE
Calabrese 'Marathon': A popular variety producing large bluish-green flower heads.

PURPLE SPROUTING
'Bordeaux': A unique purple variety not requiring cold weather to initiate flower heads, so can be harvested as early as July if sown in February.
'Claret': Large purple heads, thick stems. Late harvest from March to April.
'Early Purple Sprouting': Hardy variety. Producing spears from February to May.
'Extra Early Rudolph': Very early purple-sprouting variety producing broccoli spears from January.

WHITE SPROUTING
'Early White Sprouting': Tall white spears with 'cauliflower-like' heads from February.

Growing tips

Broccoli likes a sunny spot and good rich soil. Prepare the ground by digging over and adding some garden compost or sprinkle with fertiliser, such as Growmore, or chicken manure pellets. Brassicas like a nice firm soil to be planted in, so after digging and raking walk over the surface to firm it well before planting.

Sowing and planting

Broccoli seeds can be sown in pots or seed or cell trays or straight into the soil in a seedbed. In pots or trays, first use a multi-purpose compost or a John Innes seed or No. 1 compost. Sow the seed about 1cm/½in deep and 1cm/½in apart. When the seedlings come through, remove some to leave the remaining seedlings about 2.5cm/1in apart, or singly in cell trays. Allow to grow on and remove a few again once they get overcrowded.

When about 5cm/2in tall in a seedbed, they can be transplanted to their final situation at 60cm/2ft apart. Try to keep as much soil on the roots as possible when transplanting. Pour plenty of water into the hole as you drop in the roots. Firm the compost around the young plant well. Try to plant deep so the bottom leaves are just above the soil surface.

Plants grown in pots or trays can be planted out when they get to about 10cm/4in high.

Growing on

Unfortunately, there are many pests that can devastate brassica crops. Pigeons are one problem, so cover young plants with netting or, preferably, a fine horticultural mesh or fleece that you can buy from a garden centre or by mail order. This mesh can also prevent other pests, such as the cabbage white butterfly, from laying their eggs on the leaves. Another pest to watch out for is the flea beetle, which makes small holes in the leaves; tiny plants can be completely eaten. Whitefly and aphids

Fact file

● Calabrese is closely related to sprouting broccoli and is occasionally known as autumn broccoli. It forms one main green flower head, usually in late summer or autumn, and after cutting will produce a few smaller ones. It is sown in spring.

● Look out for the sprouting broccoli variety 'Tenderstem Green Inspiration F1', it tastes great and is packed with healthy fibre, zinc, vitamin A and glucosinolates. One floret contains as much vitamin C as an orange.

(greenfly) are a problem, too. The best care you can give the young plants is to walk the row every day quickly checking the leaves and squashing any yellow egg clusters of the cabbage white butterfly, or spraying the leaves with jets of water to remove whitefly.

Club root is a persistent fungus that causes plants to wilt and yellow, and roots to swell. Act immediately. Carefully dig up and discard infected plants. Cover the ground with construction-grade plastic for four weeks to sterilise the soil, then dig in plenty of organic matter and raise the pH, if necessary, by digging in hydrated lime.

BROCCOLI AND STILTON SOUP

Serves 4

2 tbsp oil
2 onions, chopped
2 small potatoes, peeled and diced
1 head of calabrese or large bunch of sprouting broccoli, including stalks, cut into florets
750ml/1¼pt hot vegetable or chicken stock
salt and freshly ground black pepper
250ml/5fl oz milk
100g/4oz Stilton, crumbled

1 Heat the oil in a saucepan and fry the onions and potatoes gently for 10 minutes, covered, until soft.
2 Add the broccoli and hot stock and simmer gently for 15 minutes until tender. Season with salt and pepper.
3 Lower the heat and add the milk and Stilton. Heat through gently until the cheese has melted. Allow to cool slightly, then purée.
4 Reheat and serve; garnish with a few more Stilton crumbs if you wish.

In the kitchen

Although broccoli originates from Italy, it has become a staple of the great British Sunday lunch. Broccoli is at its most nutritious and tasty if cooked soon after harvesting. The flower heads are the part that is usually eaten, but sprouting broccoli can be cut a little longer so it comes with a little leaf and stem.

Preparation and cooking: Leaves, stalks and florets can all be eaten. Simply remove dry or discoloured leaves and trim off the fibrous, tough stem base. Plunge into boiling water and boil, or steam, for about 5 minutes. The younger and fresher, the shorter the cooking time. Parboiled florets are delicious tossed in olive oil, with crushed anchovy, chillies and garlic, then stirred into pasta or risotto, or simply toss small florets into stir-fries for texture, colour and crunch.

Storage and freezing: Broccoli will keep for several days in the fridge, but avoid washing it first as this will encourage rot.

To freeze, blanch small pieces of broccoli florets in boiling water for four minutes. Remove from the heat and quickly cool in ice cold water before draining and putting in freezer bags.
♥ *High in antioxidants, iron, zinc, vitamins A and C. Broccoli is also believed to help neutralise some cancer-causing substances.*

Some broccoli plants can become top heavy, so stake them as soon as they are large enough.

When sprouting broccoli starts to produce its florets, it is ready to harvest. Occasionally one main head (similar to calabrese) will form and this should be picked to encourage smaller side shoots and flowers to grow.

Container growing

This is not an ideal crop to grow in a pot as it needs to be planted firmly and also grows quite large and tall (about 90cm/3ft). You could grow one broccoli plant in a large tub, but it would need to be staked to help keep it firm and prevent it from rocking in the wind.
It should produce enough spears for a few meals for two people and would look attractive.

Calendar

● Early Feb–Mar sowings are best made in pots or trays and grown on in a greenhouse or cold frame. Plant out Apr.
● Choose the right varieties to harvest for much of the year.

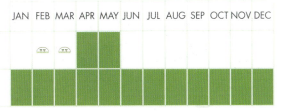

	JAN	FEB	MAR	APR	MAY	JUN	JUL	AUG	SEP	OCT	NOV	DEC
Sowing/ planting time		🌱	🌱	■	■							
Harvest time	■	■	■	■	■	■	■	■	■	■	■	■

Brussels sprouts

Varieties

'Brilliant F1': An early variety with a long harvesting period. Disease resistant and not prone to bolting.

'Cascade': Has a Royal Horticultural Society's Award of Garden Merit (AGM), meaning it performed well in trials at the RHS Garden Wisley in Surrey. Good in all weathers and resistant to mildew.

'Franklin F1': A really early sprout that is reliable and has a good flavour.

'Red Rubine': Something a bit different – a red Brussels sprout. Looks very attractive on the vegetable plot and the sprouts even keep their colour with cooking.

'Trafalgar F1': A heavy cropping variety producing firm sweet buttons.

'Valencia F1': A new variety, also with an RHS AGM. Has a purple tint to the leaves. Grows to 1m/3ft and has well-spaced buttons.

Growing tips

Sowing and planting

Preparation of the soil is best done in autumn to allow winter rains to soak and firm the soil. Prepare the ground well adding garden compost or farmyard manure. Brussels sprouts can be sown as early as February, although at this time it is best to sow them in cell trays or pots inside a warm greenhouse or on a windowsill. If you wait until March they can be sown straight into the vegetable plot in a seedbed. When sowing, use a line and make a small groove in the soil with the corner of a hoe or use the end of a stick about 1cm/½in deep. Water the drill before sowing the seed. It can be sown fairly densely, at least a seed every 5mm (¼in). Cover the seed drill with dry soil and gently firm.

Once the seedlings are through, watch out for flea beetle damage. This pest is a tiny shiny beetle that nibbles and makes holes in the

The Brussels sprout is a much maligned vegetable, probably because so many people overcook it. However, when fresh and picked small straight from the plot, then boiled lightly or stir-fried, this is a truly delicious veg. Sprouts take up a lot of space and are in the ground for months, so only consider them if you can spare the room.

Fact file

- Brussels sprouts were first cultivated in Belgium, hence being named after the capital city.
- Brussels sometimes develop 'blown' buttons, when buttons open prematurely and are loose. There are several causes for this including dryness, poor infertile soil, or the plants not being firmed in enough at planting.
- The tops of Brussels sprout plants can also be eaten.

In the kitchen

These little green gems should be enjoyed more than once a year! Brussels are best harvested small and sweet but they store well and provide nutritious greens throughout the winter.

Preparation and cooking: Peel back and discard the outer and any discoloured leaves. Brussels sprouts can then be boiled whole for five minutes in deep salty water. Drain, dot with chunks of melting butter and serve straight away, or pan fry until the leaves begin to crisp at the edges. Alternatively, they can be shredded and fried, a much tastier option. Add some chopped leeks with the shredded Brussels sprouts for a really delicious side dish. They are also tasty with crispy pancetta and toasted pine nuts, or toss with chestnuts for the Christmas table and even the kids will want to try them!

Storage and freezing: Leave the buttons on the stalk and simply twist off as many as you need.

To freeze, blanch in boiling water for three minutes, then spread out on a tray and freeze when cool. When frozen, seal in plastic bags.
♥ *High in antioxidants, vitamins A, C and B, fibre, potassium and folate.*

leaves. If spotted, put some thick glue along a piece of wood and brush over the seedlings. The flea beetles, like their name suggests, leap from the crop and will stick to the wood.

When the seedlings are large enough to handle, thin them out to about 8cm/3in apart. When they are about 10cm/4in high they can be planted out into the vegetable plot where they are to crop. Space them about 60cm/2ft apart and firm them in well.

Growing on

Newly planted sprouts will be vulnerable to attack by pigeons and other pests such as the cabbage white butterfly, so cover the young crop with horticultural fleece to keep them at bay.

Once the plants have reached a good size, it is worth staking the plants before autumn and winter because they can sometimes be bent over by windy weather. Also keep them well watered for best results.

If the crop is looking poor, give a liquid feed of a seaweed-based tonic such as Maxicrop. An extra application of a high nitrogen feed can be given up until about mid summer, but don't apply later than this or it could cause the buttons to 'blow'.

As the plants grow it is natural for some of the lower leaves to yellow and drop. Remove these and keep the plants clean and tidy.

As soon as the buttons are the right size for picking, remove the lowest ones first as and when you require them.

Container growing

Brussels sprouts are not suitable for a container, as they need plenty of space and very firm planting.

SWEET AND NUTTY SPROUTS

Serves 4

2 tbsp sunflower oil
1 onion or 3 shallots, finely chopped
350g/12oz sprouts (about 16), roughly chopped
120ml/4fl oz or a wine glass of apple juice or cider
1 tbsp sultanas
1 tsp mild curry powder
salt and freshly ground black pepper
about 20 canned sweet chestnuts, drained

1 Heat the oil in a pan and fry the onion or shallots until soft.
2 Add the sprouts and stir well, then the apple juice or cider, sultanas, curry powder and salt and pepper.
3 Cover the pan and simmer for 5 minutes.
4 Roughly chop the chestnuts, stir into the pan and continue to simmer, removing the lid to reduce the surplus liquid.

Calendar

● If sowing as early as Feb, sow indoors in pots.
● Harden off in Apr before planting out in May.
● Protect with netting against birds and consider slug control.

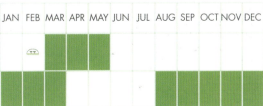

	JAN	FEB	MAR	APR	MAY	JUN	JUL	AUG	SEP	OCT	NOV	DEC
Sowing/ planting time		🌱	■	■	■							
Harvest time	■	■	■				■		■	■	■	■

Cabbages

This is another crop that has suffered from prejudice, probably caused by being served overcooked! However, if freshly cut and lightly cooked with still a bit of crunch, cabbage is delicious. A member of the brassica family, it is relatively easy to grow, although it does require attention, particularly early on, to keep pests at bay.

Varieties

RED CABBAGE
'Primero F1': Produces compact heads with great colour and not too much core. Ideal for small vegetable plots.

SAVOY CABBAGE
'Resolution F1': Produces really dark green heads. Will remain in good condition on the plot once it reaches maturity.
'Savoy King F1': A classic that is still popular today. Large, sweet-tasting cabbage.

SMOOTH BALL-HEAD
'Kilaton F1': A new variety with resistance to the disease club root, which can damage the roots and prevent growth.
'Minicole F1': A great one for the small vegetable plot. Small dense heads.
'Spring Hero F1': A really early spring cabbage if sown in July.
'Sherwood F1': A new variety producing neat 1kg/2lb heads. Good resistance to disease.

POINTED LOOSE-LEAFED CABBAGE
'Advantage F1': A great British-bred cabbage that produces 'spring greens'. It is hardy and can be sown March to October so you can eat it all year round.
'Hispi F1': Has an RHS Award of Garden Merit and is an old favourite.

JANUARY KINGS
'January King 3': An old favourite with a great flavour and very reliable.
'Robin F1': Closely related to the original 'January King'. Early to mature and produces heads about 1kg/2lb in weight.

Growing tips

Sowing and planting
It is possible to sow and harvest cabbage nearly all year round, as there are different varieties that can be sown at different times.

All cabbages like a sunny or partly sunny site and a good fertile soil. Before planting, the ground needs to be dug over and farmyard manure or garden compost added. A sprinkling of fertiliser, such as Growmore, or chicken manure pellets a week or two before sowing or planting is a good idea, too.

Sow cabbage in either a seedbed or in pots or trays in a good multi-purpose compost. Sowing in pots or cell trays is best because small seedlings are very attractive to slugs and snails.

Sow the seeds into a good multi-purpose compost. If using cell trays, put one or two seeds per cell at about 5mm/¼in deep. Water

Fact file
- Some cabbages may topple over if the ground is not firm enough, especially after a couple of frosts. In autumn, earth up the soil to the base.
- After cutting cabbage, make a cross slit in the stump that is left in the ground. Often these will sprout again, giving some extra greens for you to harvest.
- Cover with netting to protect from pigeons.

CABBAGE PIE

This is a simple dish that takes cabbage beyond being just a side dish. It is sweet and sour and delicious hot or cold.

Serves 4–6

For the pastry:
225g/8oz plain white flour
100g/4oz butter
3 tbsp water
½ tsp salt
milk to brush on top
For the filling:
275g/10oz white cabbage, sliced
1 onion, chopped
25g/1oz butter
1 apple, sliced
6 dried apricots, chopped
1 tsp ground caraway seed
3 tbsp orange juice
23cm/9in pie dish, greased

1 Preheat the oven to 200°C/400°F/gas 6/fan oven 180°C. Make the pastry by combining the pastry ingredients and rolling out to line the pie dish. Keep just under a half of the pastry for the top. Alternatively, use bought pastry.
2 Drop the cabbage into boiling water for 4 minutes and then drain.
3 Toss the onion into a frying pan with the butter and cook until soft. Add the cabbage, apple and apricot and cook for 3 more minutes.
4 Stir in the caraway and orange juice, then spoon the mixture into the pastry lined pie dish. Cover with remaining pastry, using your thumbs to seal the edges, and make two slits in the top to allow steam to escape.
5 Brush with milk and bake for 40–50 minutes.

In the kitchen

With numerous varieties of brassica arriving throughout the seasons, cabbage can be used in the kitchen all year round.

Preparation and cooking: Cabbage is not just a vegetable for boiling. It can be used raw in salads or shredded and added to mayonnaise with grated carrot to make coleslaw. Shredded cabbage can be fried or pickled. Red cabbage rapidly loses its colour and flavour during cooking. To maintain the rich purple hue and sharp bitter taste, cook with a little wine, vinegar or acidic fruit.

The smell of overcooked cabbage can be unpleasant and lingering. Cook quickly: shred, then fry or braise to prevent musty aromas escaping and retain nutrients and taste.

Storage and freezing: Store in a cool, dry place. Do not freeze.

♥ *High in antioxidants, vitamin C, iron, potassium, folate, fibre.*

well and place in a cold frame, greenhouse or on a windowsill indoors.

As soon as the seedlings are through, thin out to one seedling per cell or if sowing in seed trays lift and move the seedlings into individual pots when large enough to handle.

Growing on

When the plants are about 10cm/4in high, they can be planted outside 30–45cm/12–18in apart. Make sure you firm well around the roots, using your heel if necessary. If cabbages are planted loosely they will not produce a solid heart.

Keep the young cabbage plants free from pest attack by covering with some crop protection netting. Water the plants well and add some high nitrogen feed occasionally.

Remove any yellowing leaves and be vigilant for cabbage white butterflies. Look for yellow clusters of eggs on the underside of leaves. Remove these with thumb and finger. If left these will hatch into an army of hungry caterpillars that will reduce your cabbages to lace in no time!

Calendar

● Sow spring cabbage Jun–Aug and harvest Apr–Jun.
● Sow summer cabbage Feb–Mar and harvest Jul–Sep.
● Sow winter cabbage Apr–May and harvest Oct–Feb.

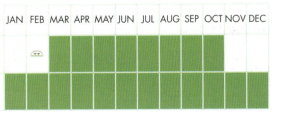

	JAN	FEB	MAR	APR	MAY	JUN	JUL	AUG	SEP	OCT	NOV	DEC
Sowing/ planting time		🌱	■	■	■	■	■	■	■	■		
Harvest time	■	■	■	■	■	■	■	■	■	■	■	■

Cauliflowers

T he cauliflower has seen a resurgence in popularity probably due to some new colours that have been introduced. Purple, and even yellow, heads (curds) are now available, making them a novelty on the vegetable plot. Cauliflower is a versatile vegetable that can be eaten raw in salads, boiled, stir-fried and pickled.

Varieties

'All The Year Round': As its name suggests it can be sown in autumn or spring to produce a long harvest.
'Andes F1': Lovely large blue-green leaves that protect the creamy white curd. Said to have a 'nutty' hint to the taste. Sow December to July; harvest May to October.
'Graffiti F1': A purple colour that intensifies with light so no need to protect the curd. Sow March to June; harvest June to October.
'Igloo': A great variety with super white curds. Sow January to May; harvest June to October.
'Lateman': Ideal for growing closer together to produce small cauliflower heads. Sow March to April; harvest July to October.
'Redoubtable F1': Produces really large heads if given the space. Sow April to June for February to March harvest.

'Regata F1': Has an RHS Award of Garden Merit. Good vigorous variety with leaves that protect the curd well. Sow May for harvesting from October to November.

Growing tips

Sowing and planting
It is possible to sow nearly all year round and have a very long harvesting period with the right varieties.

Cauliflowers like a sunny or partly sunny site and a good fertile soil that is well firmed. Prepare the ground for sowing by digging it over and adding farmyard manure or garden compost. Sprinkle with fertiliser, such as Growmore, or chicken manure pellets a week or two before sowing or planting.

Sow into either a seedbed or in pots or cell trays. Sowing in containers is preferable because small seedlings are easily damaged by pests such as slugs or flea beetles. Use a good multi-purpose compost, and sow the seeds about 5mm/¼in deep. Water well and place in a cold frame, a greenhouse, or on a windowsill indoors.

If sown in trays or pots, lift the seedlings, when large enough to handle, by their leaves and transplant individually into small pots. If you start off seedlings in cell trays, depending on the size of each cell, they may remain in these until ready for planting out.

When the plants are about 10cm/4in high, they can be planted outside about 60cm/2ft apart. Water generously and firm well around

Fact file

● When the white flower head (curd) starts to form, bend over some of the inner leaves to protect it from the sunlight.
● Cauliflower is a cool season crop. High temperatures can affect curd development.
● Club root is a troublesome disease of cauliflowers and their relatives (cabbages, Brussels sprouts and kale). New disease-resistant varieties are being developed, such as 'Clapton'.

the roots, using your heel if necessary. If cauliflowers are planted loosely they will not produce curds.

Growing on

Young cauliflowers are prone to attack from hungry pigeons, so cover the crop with netting. Once the plants are mature they are not so vulnerable.

If you use a finer netting, it will also help to keep out other pests such as the cabbage white butterfly.

If the crop is not growing well, apply a high nitrogen feed to give it a boost.

CRUNCHY BAKED CAULIFLOWER

Serves 2–4

450g/1lb cauliflower florets
4 tomatoes, peeled, seeded and chopped
salt and freshly ground black pepper to taste
2 tbsp grated Parmesan cheese
4 tbsp grated Cheddar cheese
5 tbsp dry breadcrumbs
2 tsp unsalted butter, melted

1 Preheat the oven to 180°C/350°F/gas 4/ fan oven 160°C. Steam or boil the cauliflower until slightly softened. Drain.
2 Arrange the cauliflower in a buttered shallow baking dish. Place chopped tomatoes over the florets. Season with salt and pepper.
3 Combine the cheeses in a bowl and sprinkle over the top of the cauliflower.
4 Cover with breadcrumbs and drizzle the surface with the melted butter. Bake for 20–25 minutes until golden.

In the kitchen

An attractive, delicate and subtle vegetable, cauliflower is often served bland and over cooked. If you think it's dull, take inspiration from Mediterranean and Eastern cuisine, in which the humble cauliflower is glorified and used to add texture to dishes and absorb flavours.

Preparation and cooking: To prepare, remove the tougher outer leaves and cut the stem at the base. Either tear each floret away from the stem or leave whole.

To cook, plunge in deep, boiling, salty water and boil until just tender, or caramelise florets in a little butter and a dash of white wine vinegar. Season both generously. Try mixing the cooked cauliflower florets with saffron, pine nuts and sultanas. Cauliflower's firm, waxy bite is ideal for long-cooking dishes such as casseroles, bakes and stews, and can also be used in soups and pickles and raw in salads and with dips.

Storage and freezing: Cauliflower will stay fresh in the fridge for about a week wrapped in plastic.

To freeze, break up into small sections and blanch for three minutes. Add some lemon to the water to help keep the curds white. Drain and allow to cool before placing in plastic bags.
♥ *High in antioxidants, fibre, vitamin C, vitamin A and potassium.*

Container growing

Cauliflowers are best grown in the ground as they need a good firm soil to produce quality flower heads. However, they can be grown in a very small space, so even if you have a tiny garden you could find room for a few. Some varieties, such as 'Lateman' and 'Avalanche F1', are suitable for growing in confined spaces. They can be sown and then thinned out to about 20cm/8in apart and the competition between the plants will produce compact cauliflowers with mini curds, just enough for a meal for a couple or small family.

Calendar

- For summer crops, sow under cover Jan in cell trays. Plant out late Mar for cutting Jun–Jul.
- Make another sowing Apr–May for autumn harvest.
- Sow winter varieties May–Jun.

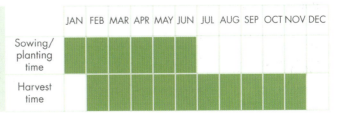

	JAN	FEB	MAR	APR	MAY	JUN	JUL	AUG	SEP	OCT	NOV	DEC
Sowing/ planting time		■	■	■	■	■						
Harvest time			■	■	■	■	■	■	■	■	■	■

Carrots

O nce all carrots were orange but now the latest trend is multi-coloured: purple, yellow and white as well as different shades of orange. However, these assorted colours of carrots are not new but a throwback. The very first carrots were white and then shades of yellow and it was the Dutch who came up with the classic orange carrot.

Varieties

Carrots can be easy to grow but not as reliable as some vegetables and so it is worth trying a few different varieties to find which one suits your soil. Carrot varieties have been developed over many years and we now have early maturing, maincrop and lates in different shapes and sizes.

The long-rooted forms have long tapering roots and are best grown in a good deep soil. Short-rooted varieties can be stumpy or even round and are great for sowing in more shallow soils or in containers.

Intermediate-rooted varieties have medium-sized roots and are the best all-rounders. They are often maincrop types and produce good carrots for storage.

'Autumn King 2': A classic late-sowing, long-rooted carrot that will remain in good condition, once mature, in the soil throughout the winter.

'Early Nantes 2': Can be sown in early March under cloches for a crop of carrots in June. It is renowned for its good length of tapering root.

'Flyaway F1': A good, sweet maincrop carrot with blunt ended roots. Has partial carrot fly resistance.

'Mokum F1': A shorter intermediate-type carrot suitable for early sowing in containers.

'Nigel F1': Long cylindrical, coreless carrots that have a good flavour. Maincrop. Also store well.

'Parmex': A great carrot for container growing as the roots are short and stumpy, almost radish shape. Also said to be good for clay soils.

'Rainbow F1': A mixture of coloured maincrop carrots including white, pale yellow and shades of orange.

'Resistafly F1': A maincrop variety that has good resistance to carrot fly.

'Sugarsnax 54 F1': A very long, narrow maincrop carrot with a sweet flavour and high in beta carotene. Ideal for grating in salads as well as for cooking.

Growing tips

Sowing and planting

Carrots are sown in rows about 15cm/6in apart. Sow thinly, leaving a gap of about 5mm/¼in between seeds if possible. The reason for this is that when you thin out the seedlings, a scent is released as you handle them, which can attract the carrot fly. Some gardeners have problems with uneven germination, which may be due to slugs eating the seedlings before they have even broken the surface, creating gaps in the rows. If this is a problem, it is better to sow more thickly and then thin out, but remove the thinnings well away to avoid attracting carrot fly. If you don't get good germination, try filling a seed drill with some multi-purpose compost and soaking this well before sowing.

Growing on

Continue to thin out carrots as they grow. As the thinnings get larger, don't throw them away –

Fact file

● Carrot fly is a troublesome pest. It lays its eggs at the base of carrot plants and the larvae tunnel into the developing roots. The damage is seen as channels in the surface of the root. Carrot fly can be prevented by covering a newly sown row with a fine mesh netting.

● Don't plant in soil that has been manured or composted in the last year or the roots will divide.

In the kitchen

Carrots are often prepared for eating by peeling first, which is a good idea if you are using carrots from the supermarket, as any traces of pesticides will be removed. Home-grown carrots do not have this problem if they are organic, and just need washing before use.
Preparation and cooking: Young and crisp, they can be chopped and eaten raw with dips or grated into salads. Older carrots, which have lost their crunch, should be cooked or used to thicken soups and stews.

Naturally high in sugars that caramelise when cooked, the addition of chopped parsley and thyme also heightens the flavour of carrots.

Pile sliced carrots into a tin lined with a large piece of foil and add a little white wine, a knob of butter and a sprig of thyme, wrap the foil over to form a parcel and bake in a hot oven for about half an hour. The carrots soak up the liquid resulting in a succulent sticky side dish. Made with wholemeal flour, brown sugar and nuts, carrot cake makes a healthy treat.
Storage and freezing: Carrots will keep for a few months in boxes of sand stored in a cool, dry shed or garage. After lifting, cut back the green tops within 5mm/¼in of the roots, and when dry place them in the boxes of sand.

To freeze, wash and dice the carrots. Blanch for three minutes and cool before putting into plastic bags or boxes and freezing. They will keep for about 12 months.

♥ *High in vitamin A, carrots also contain vitamins C, K, E, and iron, manganese, folate, potassium and calcium.*

these tiny roots are delicious. Keep the crop well watered and as the roots increase in size, they become visible above the soil. Cover them with soil when this happens, as they will turn green when exposed to the light. Unlike potatoes, this green part of the carrot is not poisonous.

Harvest when they are at the size you prefer. Maincrop carrots can be left in the ground and harvested from late summer to early autumn for good sized roots.

CARROT AND CORIANDER SOUP

Serves 4

4 medium carrots, sliced
2 potatoes, peeled and cubed
1 medium onion, chopped
1 bay leaf
1 large garlic clove, chopped
1 tbsp chopped parsley
1 tbsp chopped coriander
2 tbsp olive oil
vegetable stock cube
salt and freshly ground pepper
For the croûtons:
2 slices of thick bread (preferably a day old), in small cubes
4 tbsp olive oil
freshly chopped coriander, to serve

1 Place all the soup ingredients in a pan with 600ml/1pt water and bring to the boil. Cover the pan and simmer for 20 minutes until the carrots and potatoes are soft.
2 Discard the bay leaf and purée the soup.
3 Season to taste with salt and pepper and add 300ml/½ pt of water.
4 Make croûtons by placing the bread cubes in a pan of medium hot oil and stir and toss until crisp and golden. Drain on kitchen paper.
5 Reheat the soup before serving sprinkled with croûtons and fresh coriander.

Container growing

The short-rooted variety of carrot, such as 'Palmex' can also be grown in troughs or a large pot. Sow thinly in John Innes No. 2 compost. Keep thinning out the seedlings until there is 2.5cm/1in between them. Water well.

Calendar

- Sow early Mar under cloches.
- Sow late Mar–Jun without cloches.
- Harvest as early as Jun–Oct.

	JAN	FEB	MAR	APR	MAY	JUN	JUL	AUG	SEP	OCT	NOV	DEC
Sowing/ planting time			☷	■	■	■						
Harvest time						■	■	■	■	■		

Celeriac

With a taste like celery and easy to grow, celeriac produces knobbly swollen roots with celery-like foliage and is a lover of moist soils. In dry conditions the roots will be small, so add plenty of manure or compost to aid water retention. Celeriac doesn't suffer much from pests and disease and it stores well.

Variety

'Monarch': Good-quality creamy roots that are fairly smooth. This variety has an RHS Award of Garden Merit.

Growing tips

Sowing and planting
Sow in late February or early March in cell trays filled with multi-purpose compost. Sow two seeds per cell, water well and place on a windowsill or in a greenhouse. When the seedlings emerge remove the weakest to leave one per cell. Keep well watered.

Once the plants are a good size, start to harden them off, placing outside during the day and back in a cold frame at night. By about May/early June, after the threat of frost has passed, they can be planted outside about 30cm/12in apart and 45cm/18in between rows.

Growing on
Water the plants in well and mulch around the base with some grass cuttings to conserve moisture. When the roots have reached about 13cm/5in across, they are ready to be harvested. You can leave the roots in the ground and lift when needed. The tops will die back but you can cover the roots with straw and then fleece or netting to hold in place.

In the kitchen
The creamy white flesh has a nutty sweetness and subtle aniseed flavour.
Preparation and cooking: Expect to lose about a quarter of the weight in carving off the tough knobbly surface. Celeriac discolours very quickly after cutting, so can be prepared and stored in water with a splash of vinegar or lemon juice. It can be cooked in the same way as any root vegetable: mashed, chipped or roasted. It can also be grated raw into salads.
Storage and freezing: Store in a cool, dry place; it will keep well. Do not freeze.
♥ *Contains phosphorus, potassium and fibre.*

Container growing
Celeriac is not ideal for growing in a pot because it will dry out too quickly in summer but you could use a very large tub filled with loam-based compost.

Fact file

- A good autumn or winter crop.
- Germination can take 12 or more days.
- Mulch the crop with grass clippings from late spring to conserve moisture.

Calendar
- Keep moist to prevent bolting.
- If soil is heavy and prone to water logging, lift Oct and store in boxes of dry peat or sand.
- Celery leaf miner may attack in early summer.

	JAN	FEB	MAR	APR	MAY	JUN	JUL	AUG	SEP	OCT	NOV	DEC
Sowing/ planting time		🌱	🌱		■	■						
Harvest time									■	■		

This popular salad and cooking vegetable likes moist soil, so grow it on a free-draining site enriched with plenty of compost or manure. The traditional method of growing celery involves earthing up the stems as they grow to blanch them. Fortunately, we have better self-blanching varieties today that do not require so much work.

Varieties

'Galaxy' ('Lathom Self Blanching'): Good-quality tender stems. Not prone to bolting. This variety has an RHS Award of Garden Merit.
'Victoria F1': Upright stems that are crunchy and tasty. It also has an RHS Award of Garden Merit and has good bolt resistance.

Growing tips

Sowing and planting

Sow in March in cell trays filled with a multi-purpose compost. Sow one seed per cell, water well and place in a cold frame or a greenhouse to grow on. In May or early June, plant outside in rows. Self-blanching varieties of celery are planted 23cm/9in apart. If growing the older trench varieties, dig a trench about 30cm/12in deep and add manure to the bottom, cover with soil and plant the celery about 15cm/6in deep.

Growing on

Water the plants in well and make sure that the soil never dries out. Give a liquid feed of a general-purpose fertiliser once a week during the summer.

In August remove the lower leaves and side shoots of the trench varieties and surround the stalks with some cardboard, leaving the leaves just poking out of the top. Start to fill in the trench around the stems to blanch them.

Fact file

- Self-blanching celery can be grown in a block to help with the blanching process.
- Finish harvesting self-blanching celery before the first frosts arrive. The trench types have better protection so can be lifted right up to Christmas and beyond if mild.

In the kitchen

Slender stems add a flavoursome base to casseroles and soups, with a hint of aniseed, when cooked slowly, and when raw gives a crisp texture to cold dishes and salads – the sprouting leafy tops are delicious in salads, too.
♥ *High in fibre, potassium; lowers blood pressure.*

Calendar

- Best sown under cover in pots or trays in Mar.
- Planted out from end May.
- Make direct sowings Apr–May.
- Squash leaf miner larvae on the leaves in summer.

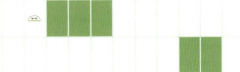

	JAN	FEB	MAR	APR	MAY	JUN	JUL	AUG	SEP	OCT	NOV	DEC
Sowing/planting time			🕶	■	■	■						
Harvest time										■	■	

Chicory

Chicories are a popular Italian salad crop but they have never really taken off in the UK. One reason could be their slightly bitter taste, but they should be more widely grown for the zing they can add to salads. They make a great addition to a mixed salad, combined with some more subtle-tasting leaves.

Varieties

There are two types of chicory. One is the 'Witloof' chicory that is familiar as the white, green-tipped chicons (hearts), known as endive in Europe and the US. These are achieved by 'forcing' and are a little trickier to grow. The other chicories are similar to lettuce and are either green or red leaved (radicchio).

'Palla Rossa': A forcing or non-forcing type that forms a pretty ball-head of red leaves. Not hardy.

'Sugar Loaf': Also called 'Pain de Sucre', it is a non-forcing type.

'Witloof': This is the classic forcing variety. Best forced by covering completely with compost to keep the chicons pale.

Growing tips

Sowing and planting

Sow seed outside in shallow seed drills about 1cm/½in deep in rows about 30cm/12in apart. Water well and when germinated, thin out the seedlings. As they grow keep thinning out when necessary.

Growing on

Keep the crop well watered and thin until plants are 15cm/6in apart (forcing types) or 30cm/12in apart (non-forcing types).

In autumn the forcing types should be cut back to just above soil level. At this stage the plants can be lifted, replanted in pots of John Innes No. 2 compost and placed in a greenhouse or cold frame. Keep the stems covered and in darkness. In spring when the chicons are about 15cm/6in high they can be cut for the table.

Container growing

Chicory will grow well in containers and the foliage of the red-leafed varieties provides a lovely contrast with other veg, bringing colour to the patio. Just two or three plants in a large tub would suffice.

Fact file

- Forced chicory is grown from the roots that are cut down in autumn and grown in a dark, cool but frost-free place.

Calendar

- Protect in mid winter with open-ended cloches.
- Sow forcing types May–Jun. Sow non-forcing types Jun–Jul.
- Harvest forcing types Feb–Apr and non-forcing types Sep–Jan.

	JAN	FEB	MAR	APR	MAY	JUN	JUL	AUG	SEP	OCT	NOV	DEC
Sowing/ planting time					■	■	■					
Harvest time	■	■	■						■	■	■	■

Courgettes – and also marrows – have to be the first choice for beginners to vegetable growing. They grow quickly and produce masses of fruit without too much trouble. As a bonus, they are really attractive plants with big leaves and stunning yellow flowers that can also be eaten, especially lightly battered and deep-fried!

Varieties

'Cavili F1': This variety produces very pale green fruits and is parthenocarpic, meaning it will produce fruit even if the flowers are not pollinated. It is said to have a creamier flesh texture than the more usual dark-skinned courgettes.
'Defender F1': Produces excellent yields if you keep cutting the fruits.
'Kojac F1': If you don't like harvesting courgettes because of their prickly stems then grow this one. It has an open habit and hardly any spines.
'Orelia F1': Long yellow fruits on vigorous plants. Good disease resistance.
'Parthenon F1': This is also parthenocarpic, but is the more usual dark green type.

Growing tips

Sowing and planting
Courgettes and marrows are tender vegetables so are usually sown in containers and kept in warm conditions until planting out at the end of May or the beginning of June.

Fact file

- Work has been done to create varieties resistant to the cucumber mosaic virus, a disease that stunts the plants and turns the leaves a mottled yellow.
- Courgettes and marrows come in trailing and bush forms, although bush forms are more popular for courgettes.

- Keep harvesting courgettes while still small to encourage more flowers and fruit.
- Watch out for slugs – they love courgettes.

Use either large-celled seed trays, or small 9cm/3½in pots, filled with a multi-purpose or a John Innes seed or No. 1 compost, and sow one seed per cell or pot. Place the pots on a warm windowsill or in a propagator.

Check them daily, as they are very quick to germinate. If too warm, the stems stretch very quickly, making them top heavy. Once they have germinated, move to cooler conditions, such as the greenhouse or a cold frame, to grow on. Watch out for slugs as courgettes are a particular favourite of theirs.

When all danger of frost has passed, by about the end of May/beginning of June, the courgettes and marrows can be planted outside.

Growing on
Courgettes and marrows like a fertile soil. Some gardeners grow them on old muck heaps, which is fine if the manure is old. New manure heaps will be too 'hot' in terms of temperature and richness and may scorch the leaves.

In your plot, dig a 30cm/1ft deep hole with a similar diameter and fill with garden compost or well-rotted manure. Then heap a half mix of soil and compost into the hole to form a mound. Plant the courgette or marrow into a hole at the top. Make sure you plant deep enough to support the stem. Sometimes they can be a bit floppy at this stage so, if necessary, tie the stem to a small stake. One problem after planting is wind battering the young plants, shredding the leaves and snapping the weak stems.

Container growing

You can grow a courgette or marrow plant in a large pot – either a large bucket size or even better a 60cm/2ft diameter container. Fill the pot with a mix of multi-purpose compost and

some garden compost if you have it. Plant one courgette plant only in this size container and place in a warm sunny spot. Keep the plant well watered, especially once the fruits begin to form.

In the kitchen

Marrows and courgettes are as redolent of summer as tomatoes and equally as good in salads or pasta dishes. Courgettes are best cut when small, ideally when only 10–13cm/4–5 in long. If you have several plants you will find that you can be picking fruits every day. If the courgettes are left to grow into marrows, the plants tend to stop flowering as much, resulting in a reduced crop.

Preparation and cooking: Old marrows can become hollow, seedy and bitter. The tastiest flesh is close to the skin, so dry centres can be removed. The flowers are edible and a real gourmet treat; a delicacy stuffed with soft cheese and deep-fried. The fresh, mild flavours are perfect with seasonal soft green herbs such as mint, basil and parsley.

Rinse courgettes thoroughly, top and tail then slice as required. Eat raw in salads or steam, roast or soften in a little butter and toss with pasta. Courgettes are great simply sliced and fried in butter. Courgettes and marrows also make great wine, jam or pickle and chutney. Stuffed marrow is another popular dish. The fruits are cut into sections, the centre scooped out and filled with part-cooked mince, onion and tomato, or other ingredients to taste, and then baked.

Storage ands freezing: Courgettes and marrows will store in a fridge for about a week, but this crop is such a prolific producer of fruits during the height of the season you can harvest and eat fresh fruits daily.

Courgettes can be frozen, but marrows are not as suitable. Small courgettes can be sliced and blanched for a couple of minutes before removing and draining off excess water. Pat dry with some kitchen towel before placing in bags and freezing. If you open freeze them on trays first, before putting into bags, they won't stick together.

♥ *High in vitamins A,C and E.*

COURGETTE AND SLOW-ROASTED GARLIC SOUP

Serves 2

3 garlic cloves in their skins
1 tbsp olive oil
1 onion, chopped
2 stalks of celery, chopped
5 courgettes, sliced
¼ tsp nutmeg
750ml/25fl oz stock
salt and freshly ground pepper

1 Roast the garlic cloves in their skins with a little of the oil in a preheated oven (150°C/300°F/gas 2/fan oven 130°C) for 30 minutes, checking occasionally to make sure they don't burn.
2 Meanwhile, heat the remaining oil in a saucepan, fry the onion and celery for 2 minutes, then add the courgettes and nutmeg. Stir-fry for about 5 minutes.
3 Remove the garlic from the oven, peel and add to the pan along with the stock. Bring to the boil and simmer for 20 minutes, or until all the ingredients have softened, then blend. Season to taste.
Serve with: Chunky slices of granary bread.

Calendar

● Sow direct outside May–Jun.
● Sow seed on its side at 2.5cm/1in deep to help drain off water.
● Planting on a mound helps water drain from the middle of the plant.

	JAN	FEB	MAR	APR	MAY	JUN	JUL	AUG	SEP	OCT	NOV	DEC
Sowing/planting time					■	■						
Harvest time							■	■	■	■	■	

Cucumbers

The traditional long, smooth varieties need to be grown in a warm, almost hot, humid atmosphere such as greenhouse or polytunnel conditions. Some of the smaller-fruited more prickly types can be grown outside. Many of the greenhouse varieties available are now all-female plants, which means there are no male flowers to remove.

Varieties

The old-fashioned varieties produce male and female flowers on the same plant and if the female flowers are pollinated by pollen from the male flowers, the resulting fruit are often bitter. Some of the outdoor types still produce male and female flowers, but don't need the male flowers removing.

'Carmen F1': An all-female variety that has an RHS Award of Garden Merit. It also has good disease resistance and fruits are produced in profusion.

'Cupino': Another all-female variety that produces very small cucumbers. It is best in a greenhouse but can be grown outside.

'Long White': A pure white form that can be grown outside. It has a thin skin and so peeling is not necessary. Do not remove male flowers.

'Swing': A new variety that is good for indoors and out. The fruits are slightly prickly and about 20cm/8in long.

Growing tips

Sowing and planting

Sow seeds about 1cm/½in deep in multi-purpose compost in small individual 9cm/3½in pots or in cell trays. Water well and place in a propagator at 24°C/75°F. It is important for cucumbers to have good warm conditions to germinate.

Once the seedlings are through, reduce the temperature slightly and place in a well-lit spot to grow on. If sowing in February grow on indoors at no lower than 15°C/60°F. If you want to grow on in a greenhouse at this time of year, some heat will be required. Sow in April if your greenhouse is not heated.

The plants may need potting on into 13cm/5in pots once they outgrow their small pots.

Keep in warm conditions at this stage to encourage new growth.

Growing on

By about May the plants will be ready for transplanting in the greenhouse, either into the borders or preferably into a special raised bed filled with layers of manure and sterilised soil or compost. Or in growbags – the compost is perfect for cucumbers. The problem with growing directly in the greenhouse border is the possible build up of disease.

Outdoor varieties can be planted out in June into soil earthed up in mounds with plenty of farmyard manure or garden compost incorporated. The outdoor ones are usually best left to trail along the ground but the greenhouse cucumbers should be tied upright to wires or canes. Use soft string to tie up the stems on a regular basis to keep them well supported.

Feed the plants weekly with a high nitrogen feed, such as dried blood or a general-purpose feed. Once the growing tip of the plant has

Fact file

- The female flowers can be recognised by the bulge just behind the flower.
- Male flowers have no bulge and have stamens bearing the powdery yellow pollen.
- Plants may produce more fruit than they can carry and as a result will often drop them prematurely. Maintain feeding and watering and the situation should soon right itself again.

reached the greenhouse roof, remove it. The side shoots growing off the main stem will bear the female flowers. These can also be 'stopped' by removing the growing tip about two leaves beyond a female flower. This will encourage all the plant's energy to go into swelling the fruit.

Keep the greenhouse well ventilated on hot sunny days and dampen down the floor regularly as cucumbers love a humid atmosphere.

Container growing

Cucumbers can be grown individually in 25cm/10in diameter pots, filled with John Innes No. 3 compost, or two to a growbag. The cucumbers will still need the support of a framework of canes. It may be useful to place the growbags or pots against a fence or wall and secure the plants with string. Sow the appropriate variety to avoid the collapse of stems when the plants are large. Water often to maintain growth.

CUCUMBER WITH CREAM CHEESE AND BLACK PEPPER SANDWICHES

low-fat cream cheese
good quality wholemeal or granary bread, sliced and crusts removed
freshly ground black pepper
cucumber, thinly sliced
cress to garnish

1 Generously spread the cream cheese onto the bread.
2 Grind plenty of black pepper over the cream cheese and top with the cucumber slices.
3 Layer double-decker style and garnish with cress. Cut into fingers and eat immediately.

In the kitchen

Cucumber is loved for its crispness and fresh flavour and is a favourite for summer salads. It is best harvested when the cucumbers are small, especially the outdoor variety, which can become a bit leathery if left on the plant too long.

Preparation and cooking: Skin can be tough and bitter, so it's best removed before use. Peel the tough, stringy, green fibres off with a serrated peeler. To reduce the water content, slice the cucumber lengthways and scoop out the watery seeds with a teaspoon. Seeds make dressings run and sandwiches soggy.

Cucumber is refreshing sliced thinly in salads and delicious with summer herbs, especially mint and dill. Diced and mixed with a little soured cream or yogurt, with dill and garlic, it makes a tasty dip. Chill peeled cubes of cucumber in the fridge or freezer. They are mostly water, so frost over quickly and can be dropped into drinks instead of ice. Cucumber can also be enjoyed hot: peel and dice, then fry in hot butter until just soft. Season to taste and enjoy with fish or in salads and soups.

Storage and freezing: In a fridge cucumbers will store for a week or more. They are not suited to freezing as they become mushy when thawed.
♥ *High in potassium and silicon, which helps keep tendons and ligaments healthy, the green skin is rich in carotenoid antioxidants.*

Calendar

- Sow Feb–Mar under cover.
- Plant in the greenhouse Apr–May.
- Plant outside varieties May–Jun after the frosts, but watch out for slugs.

	JAN	FEB	MAR	APR	MAY	JUN	JUL	AUG	SEP	OCT	NOV	DEC
Sowing/ planting time		�	⌒	⌒	⌒	■						
Harvest time						■	■	■	■	■		

Endive can be curly or broad leaved and is a popular salad crop in Italy and other European countries. In the UK, many ready-prepared salad mixes include endive, which has a bitter taste and is very lettuce-like. But it can be confusing because what we know as chicory (see page 30) is called endive in Europe and the US.

Varieties

'Cornet de Bordeaux': Has loose upright heads and is very hardy.
'Cuor D'oro Pancalieri': Also called endive 'Golden Heart'. Has tight heads of frilly leaves. Sow mid summer for harvesting in autumn.
'Frisée Glory': Produces a mass of narrow divided leaves that form a dense heart, or alternatively pick the baby leaves when required.
'Manos': An early curled-leaf type ideal for summer and autumn cropping.

Fact file

- Keep the soil moist for spring-sown endive as a hot dry summer may cause the plants to bolt.
- Sow short rows of endive every month to get a succession of heads from summer through to autumn and winter.
- Young leaves of endive will be less bitter so can be harvested when small. Sow seed thinly and use seedlings in a salad.

Growing tips

Sowing and planting

The spring-sown endive will tolerate a little shade during the day but the summer and early autumn sown ones are best given a sunny position. Endive prefers a light soil that does not dry out too quickly. Heavy clay provides the worst conditions.

Sow seeds fairly thickly in rows 5mm/¼in deep at about 30cm/12in apart. Thin out the seedlings to about 23cm/9in apart and remove any weed growth. Keep them well watered – especially important with summer sowings. Plants that are put under stress even when small will bolt.

Growing on

Once the plants reach a good size, blanch one or two by gathering up the outside leaves to a point around the top of the plant and tying together with string. Alternatively, the short frilly-leaved ones are best covered with a flowerpot over the centre of the plant. Cover the holes up in the bottom of the pot with some black tape as you want to exclude all light. Check the plants

In the kitchen

A milder cousin of chicory with a clean and refreshing bite and pretty lacy tips, the colourful tinted leaves are attractive but bitter.

Preparation and storage: Pick off the best outer leaves for use whole. The blanched leaves are tastier and are a good addition to mixed salads, prepared in the same way as lettuce. If the leaves are too bitter, soak them in cold, salted water for half an hour or wash them in warm water. A good salad dressing sweetened with sugar, honey or balsamic vinegar will also help counteract the bitterness. Endive can be quickly stir-fried and added to pasta dishes.

Storage and freezing: Store in a cool, dark place, any sweetness will diminish quickly after harvest. It is not suitable for freezing but will keep for a couple of days in the fridge.

♥ *A good source of vitamin E, phosphorus, fibre, vitamins A, K and C plus many other minerals.*

ENDIVE AND CHICORY SALAD

Serves 2

For the dressing:
1 tbsp walnut oil
3 tbsp sunflower oil
2 tsp Dijon mustard
3 tbsp white wine vinegar
1 tsp sugar
2 tsp lemon juice
salt and freshly ground pepper
For the salad:
walnut pieces to garnish
endive and chicory leaves
25g/1oz blue cheese, grated or chopped

1 Whisk together the salad dressing ingredients.
2 Toast the walnut pieces in a pan for about 5 minutes. Wash and dry the salad leaves and put in a bowl.
3 Sprinkle over the grated cheese and the toasted walnuts, then drizzle over the dressing.
Serve with: Crusty bread

about three weeks later and you should have some almost white leaves for harvesting. This may take a bit longer in the winter months, although the winter types are not usually as bitter.

Cut endives as you would a lettuce, slicing through the stem below the head. If you leave a stump they may regrow giving a second harvest.

Container growing

Endive can be grown in containers and is an attractive plant, especially the curly-leaved types. Use a large pot at least 45cm/18in diameter for two or three plants, filled with a John Innes No. 2 or 3 compost.

Calendar

- Sow directly into the soil in Sept but cover with cloches to keep the worst of the weather off them.
- Sow Apr–Sep.
- Harvest Jul–Feb.

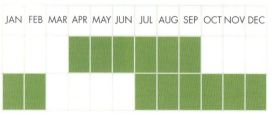

	JAN	FEB	MAR	APR	MAY	JUN	JUL	AUG	SEP	OCT	NOV	DEC
Sowing/ planting time				■	■	■	■	■	■			
Harvest time	■	■					■	■	■	■	■	■

French beans

French beans are a great choice for newcomers to vegetable growing, especially for those with little space. Even just one plant will produce many beans over a long period if picked regularly. There are two types, climbing and dwarf, mostly with cylindrical pods but you can grow varieties with flat pods and in different colours.

Varieties

CLIMBING FRENCH BEANS

'Cobra': A heavy-yielding climbing bean with round green pods about 18cm/7 in long. Lovely mauve flowers.

'Goldfield': A wonderful yellow flat-podded type. The beans don't have that stringy edge to them and, at 25cm/10in long, are great value. Attractive in the flower border.

DWARF FRENCH BEANS

'Borlotto': There is a tall, climbing version of this one too. Picked young the green beans are lovely and tender. Alternatively, wait until the pods mature turning a fiery red and streaked with cream. The seeds can be used in stews or soups.

'Delinel': Producing masses of thin round pods, this is an amazing cropper continuing for as long as you keep harvesting them. Plants are sturdy and remain upright, too.

'Purple Teepee': Produces wonderful purple pods that turn green when cooked.

Growing tips

Sowing and planting

French beans are not fully hardy so make early sowings indoors in pots or cell trays. Use multi-purpose compost and sow four beans to a 9cm/3½in pot or one seed per cell if using cell trays. Just hold one end of the seed and insert into the compost about 2.5cm/1in deep. Cover with more compost, water well and place in a propagator or on a warm windowsill.

It will take seven to ten days for the seedlings to emerge. If the seeds are in a propagator, remove as soon as you see the seedlings breaking through the surface. They will stretch and go leggy if left in the heat for too long. Place on a sunny windowsill or in a greenhouse.

Growing on

Choose a sunny spot to plant your beans and prepare the ground by digging in plenty of well-rotted garden compost or farmyard manure. A sprinkling of fertiliser or chicken manure is a good idea too, as French beans like a rich soil.

By early to mid May the pots of beans can be placed in a sheltered part of the garden or in a cold frame to get used to cooler temperatures. Protect plants from any late frosts with fleece. By the end of May, beginning of June, plant out into the vegetable plot. Climbing

Fact file

- Dwarf beans grow to about 30cm/12in high. The climbing ones can top 2m/7ft in a season.
- It takes about 8–10 weeks between sowing and harvesting.
- If you have had problems producing a good runner bean crop, try climbing French beans.

beans will already be quite tall, so put your canes or poles in place first and then plant one or two plants next to each support. Tie the stem to the pole loosely to encourage the bean to grow up that support. You will need to use slug control at this stage.

Space dwarf beans about 15cm/6in apart in rows about 45cm/18in apart. Water the plants well during dry spells. Once the beans are about 8cm/3in long start harvesting, they are better when picked small, and it will encourage more to grow.

Container growing

French beans can easily be grown in containers, especially the dwarf types. A large pot with a diameter of about 30cm/12in could hold two to three plants quite happily. Use John Innes No. 3 compost and keep well watered, especially when the beans start to form. During the growing season give the plants a feed with a general-purpose liquid feed and harvest the beans regularly to keep the plants producing more flowers.

CHILLI-SPICED BEANS

Serves 4

450g/1lb French beans, trimmed and sliced
2 tbsp olive oil
1 tsp mustard seeds
2 fresh green chillies, seeds removed and finely chopped
1 garlic clove, peeled and chopped
salt and freshly ground black pepper
some chopped chives or spring onion leaves
pine nuts to garnish (optional)

1 Boil the beans until almost cooked.
2 Heat the oil in a pan and fry the mustard seeds until they crackle. Lower the heat and add the chillies and garlic. Stir in the beans and season.
3 Snip the chives or leaves and add to the beans. Garnish with pine nuts, if using, and serve.

In the kitchen

These tender vegetables are crunchy, sweet and refreshing raw, but subtle and earthy once cooked. It is always best to use small beans as these are the most tender and the tastiest. If necessary, rather than leave large beans on the plant, remove and compost them to encourage more flowers and fresh young beans to form. If you wish to save the beans for the seeds then keep a row specifically for this purpose and once mature the pods can be shelled and the beans dried for winter use.

Preparation and cooking: French beans are usually prepared for eating by pinching off the top of the bean. The flat-podded beans, especially if they have grown quite large, may be stringy so the edges of the beans need to be peeled off using a sharp knife before cutting into sections. You can use them raw to add crunch to salads, or toss into pasta or stir-fries. To cook, quickly blanch in fast boiling, salted water and serve immediately. Plunge into cold water to refresh if using chilled in salads.

Storage and freezing: These delicate thin beans lose sweetness rapidly, even in cold storage. Pick, wash and slice as required for peak flavour and bite.

To freeze, wash the beans and cut off the stalk ends. Cut up into smaller sections if long. Blanch for two to three minutes before cooling and putting in plastic bags or boxes and freezing. They will keep for about 12 months.
♥ *High in vitamins A, K and C and folate.*

Calendar

- Sow under cover Mar–Apr.
- Sow outside late Apr–May once out of danger of frosts that could damage the emerging shoots.
- Harvest Jun–Oct.

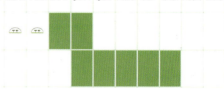

	JAN	FEB	MAR	APR	MAY	JUN	JUL	AUG	SEP	OCT	NOV	DEC
Sowing/ planting time			☻	☻	■	■						
Harvest time						■	■	■	■	■		

Yyou either love garlic or you hate it but, whatever your view, this crop is certainly a popular one and until you have tasted your own you won't believe that it can be so much better than shop bought. It isn't a difficult crop to grow, but it is in the ground for a long time, so it is best grown in a sunny corner of your garden.

Varieties

'Albigensian Wight': A large garlic from the southern region of France.
'Elephant garlic': A massive, mild bulb great for roasting whole.
'Purple Wight': Has very chunky cloves and is slightly sweet.
'Solent Wight': Very large bulbs about 6cm/2½in across. Keeps well.

Growing tips

Planting

Autumn is the best time to plant garlic because it actually benefits from a period of cold to induce good hearty bulb formation by summer. Garlic bulbs can be bought in early autumn from garden centres or by mail order from specialist growers. To plant, split up the bulbs into individual cloves and plant with the pointed end uppermost. Bury them about 5cm/2in deep and 15cm/6in apart.

If your soil is very heavy you may want to wait until February to plant or add some gritty sand to the trench before planting.

Growing on

If planted in October/November, the garlic should be showing shoots by January. In spring a high nitrogen feed can be beneficial to encourage good growth.

Between May and June, the leaves will start to yellow and growth will cease. Once the foliage has withered it is time to lift the bulbs. Choose a period of settled dry weather to do this and leave the bulbs on the surface of the soil to dry for a day.

Fact file

- Garlic was used in ancient Egypt and in classical Greece and Rome.
- Originating from central Asia there are two types – hardneck, also known as rocambole or serpent garlic owing to the shape of the flower spike, and softnecks (*Allium sativum*).
- Store cloves in an open container or weave into ropes to hang in a cool, frost-free place.

Calendar

- Plant Oct–Feb.
- An application of sulphur in spring is said to increase the compound that gives garlic its renowned medicinal properties.
- Harvest Jun–Jul.

	JAN	FEB	MAR	APR	MAY	JUN	JUL	AUG	SEP	OCT	NOV	DEC
Sowing/ planting time	■	■								■	■	■
Harvest time						■	■					

Container growing

Garlic can be grown in large pots. Use John Innes No. 3 compost, with some added grit for drainage. Do not overfeed – there is already some fertiliser in the compost when purchased – as the growth of the bulbs may become too soft and lush, making them vulnerable to rotting diseases.

Keep the compost moist, but be careful not to over water. As growth slows down reduce watering to allow the bulbs to ripen.

In the kitchen

A vital ingredient in the kitchen, garlic adds flavour and depth to all savoury dishes. Although bitter and pungent when raw, cooking enhances the natural sweetness and reduces acidity.
Preparation and cooking: Always remove any green shoots running through the centre, they are bitter and indigestible.

Garlic is an acquired taste and you may wish to reduce the number of cloves given in a recipe at first. The finer the cloves are chopped, the stronger they will taste, so if you do not wish the flavour to be overpowering, roughly chop or use whole cloves in your cooking. For a stronger taste, crush the cloves. You can buy a garlic crusher for this or simply place the cloves on a chopping board and crush with the flat of a wide-bladed knife, pushed down with your palm. Crushed cloves can be used raw in dressing or cooked in a base for sauces, soups and stews. It is also wonderful roasted whole. Simply slice the top off and wrap each bulb individually in tin foil and bake in a hot oven for half an hour.
Storage and freezing: Store in a cool, dry place. There is no need to freeze.
♥ *Good antiseptic and antiviral properties; reduces cholesterol.*

GAZPACHO

This cold soup started as a simple, sustaining meal for workers in the vineyards of Spain, and was based not on tomatoes, but stale bread, water, oil and any vegetables available at the time. Today, gazpacho makes a truly refreshing dish on a warm day and is a great way to use up those excess cucumbers and tomatoes.

Serves 4
1 large cucumber, peeled and finely chopped
1 green pepper, deseeded and finely chopped
1 onion, finely chopped
6 tomatoes, peeled and finely chopped
4 garlic cloves, crushed
juice of ½ lemon
60ml/2fl oz olive oil
½ tsp chilli powder
½ tsp shredded fresh basil, plus a few whole leaves to garnish
salt
pinch of ground cumin
600ml/1pt tomato juice or the equivalent in blended, peeled fresh tomatoes

1 Place the cucumber, pepper, onion and tomatoes in a large bowl. Add the garlic and the remaining ingredients and mix well. Season to taste.
2 Place in the fridge overnight before serving. Garnish with some fresh basil leaves.
3 If you prefer, the soup can be completely puréed, or served with a little of the finely chopped vegetables added to each bowl.

Kale, or borecole, is one of the best winter greens you can grow and packed with health-giving nutrients. It is a member of the brassica family, so is closely related to cabbages and broccoli, but is probably a little easier to grow. It is hardy and will do well in most soils, although a more limey soil is preferable to an acidic one.

Varieties

'Black Tuscany' ('Nero di Toscana'): Produces very long, slender, crinkly, deep green leaves. A wonderful flavour. Can also be harvested when really small as salad leaves.

'Redbor F1': A stunning variety with heavily crinkled purple-red leaves. Green kale and 'Redbor' planted alternately will make a stunning show.

'Red Russian': A flatter leaf, with a curly edge. Has good flavour, especially after frost.

'Reflex F1': Good-sized plants with very curly dark green leaves. Has RHS Award of Garden Merit.

'Starbor F1': A very crinkly green variety that is ideal for growing closely together, so good for a small area.

Growing tips

Sowing and planting

Kale likes a sunny, or partly sunny, site and a good fertile soil. When preparing to sow or plant, the ground needs to be dug over and a sprinkling of fertiliser or chicken manure pellets applied.

Kale can be sown quite thickly straight into a seedbed at 2cm/¾in deep in March. Thin out the seedlings as they grow to leave space between plants. When they get to 10cm/4in high, transplant them in their final position in rows about 45cm/18in apart. If you are planting kale after a crop of early potatoes or peas, remove all the debris, dig over, then firm by walking over it before planting.

Kale can also be sown in pots or cell trays in a greenhouse or on a windowsill. Plant out when all danger of frost has passed.

Growing on

When planting make sure you firm well around the roots. Keep the young kale plants free from pest attack by covering with fine mesh netting. Keep the plants well watered and add some high nitrogen feed occasionally. Remove any

Fact file

- Pick young leaves, older leaves can be bitter.
- Seeds will germinate in about a week.
- In winter, kale is one of the most productive crops you can grow.
- Apply fertiliser in spring around winter kale to boost growth for a second crop.
- Cover young plants with crop protection fleece to deter birds, whitefly and cabbage white butterflies.

yellowing leaves and be vigilant for whitefly under the surface of the leaves. Keep the plants weed free and firm the soil around the stems periodically, to prevent wind rock.

Once the plants have reached a decent size you can start harvesting the leaves. Choose ones near the top but avoid taking out the very growing tip of the plant.

Container growing

Kale makes an attractive show in a large container. In the picture, a silver trough sets off some plants of 'Black Tuscany' mixed with purple-pink chives. A 60cm/2ft diameter container or trough with a similar depth is best. This is less likely to dry out easily. Fill with John Innes No. 3 compost and mix in some garden compost if you have it. Two or three kale plants could be grown in this size of container, especially the smaller compact types such as 'Starbor'.

SESAME KALE

Serves 6
450g/1lb kale
10ml/2 tsp sesame seed oil
2 garlic cloves, crushed
2 tsp water
1 tsp soy sauce
2 tsp toasted sesame seeds
salt and freshly ground black pepper

1 Wash the kale and remove any tough stems. Tear the kale leaves into bite-sized sections.
2 Heat the sesame seed oil in a frying pan or skillet and stir in the garlic. Add the kale and water and cook, covered, for a minute. Remove the lid and stir the kale, to coat with the oil and garlic.
3 Continue cooking for another 2 minutes before stirring in the soy sauce and sesame seeds. Season with pepper and salt, if needed but taste it first as it may be quite salty. Serve immediately.

In the kitchen

One of the few greens whose blue tinged leaves are at their most tender and flavoursome during the sparse winter months. Kale is a delicious vegetable if harvested and cooked correctly. Small young leaves are the tastiest and are best after a frost.

Preparation and cooking: Discard dry or discoloured leaves. Fold the leaves in half along the stalk, lay flat on a chopping board and cut or tear the stalk away Wash thoroughly and shred.

The leaves can be boiled as you would cabbage, but don't overcook. They are ready after about five minutes, when the leaves start to soften and are still a deep green colour. Steaming is a good method of cooking, too. You can also toss leaves in a large frying pan with a tablespoon of water and cover with a lid. Kale is a good alternative to cabbage in stews.

Storage and freezing: Kale will keep for about three days in the fridge.

To freeze, blanch washed leaves and shoots for one minute. Drain and cool and then chop and place in freezer bags.

♥ High in antioxidants, vitamin A and C, iron, potassium, folate, fibre.

Calendar

● You can harvest kale sown in the spring right through the winter.
● After frost or windy weather, firm down the roots to prevent root damage.

	JAN	FEB	MAR	APR	MAY	JUN	JUL	AUG	SEP	OCT	NOV	DEC
Sowing/ planting time			■	■	■							
Harvest time	■	■	■								■	■

Kohlrabi

This vegetable should be more popular in the UK because it is fast maturing and not too difficult to grow. It is a member of the brassica family but it is the swollen base of the stem that is harvested and eaten, either boiled whole or chopped up – it is not a root vegetable. The leaves are also tasty eaten after boiling for a short time.

Varieties

'Lanro': A reliable green variety with a lovely flavour for use in stews, soups or raw in coleslaw and salads.

'Purple Danube F1': This is said to be one of the best purple varieties to grow. The globes are sweet and can be eaten raw in salads.

Growing tips

Sowing and planting

Kohlrabi is best sown direct in the ground in rows 30cm/12in apart. Sow the seeds about 5mm/¼in apart and when the seedlings emerge thin them out to about 2.5cm/1in apart and then again as they grow to about 15cm/6in apart.

Fact file

- Kohlrabi is a suitable crop for light sandy soils.
- The name comes from the German meaning 'cabbage turnip' and it is a popular vegetable in Germany.

Growing on

Keep the rows of kohlrabi free from weeds and check the leaves for signs of pests. Pigeons may be a problem pecking the leaves so cover with netting or put up some bird scarers.

In times of drought, give the soil a good soaking once a week.

Container growing

Kohlrabi can be grown in a container as it is not deep rooted. A trough planted up with both green- and purple-coloured varieties would make an attractive and useful display, as you can eat the leaves, too.

In the kitchen

With its mild flavour, this delicious vegetable can be eaten raw or cooked in stews, soups or stir-fries. It is delicious with honey. The leaves and stems can also be eaten, after boiling until tender.

Preparation and cooking: Peel and chop the kohlrabi, then cook in a saucepan with a chopped carrot and enough chicken or vegetable stock just to cover for about eight minutes until tender. Add a sprinkling of chopped parsley, a squeeze of lemon juice, a knob of butter and 2 tbsp of honey. Stir over a high heat for two minutes to reduce.

Storage and freezing: Store in a cool, dry place. Do not freeze.

♥ High in vitamin C, potassium and fibre.

Calendar

- Kohlrabi will remain in good condition for quite a while once mature.
- It is best harvested when it has grown to between golf ball and tennis ball size.

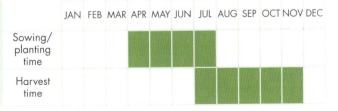

	JAN	FEB	MAR	APR	MAY	JUN	JUL	AUG	SEP	OCT	NOV	DEC
Sowing/ planting time				■	■	■						
Harvest time							■	■	■	■	■	

Leeks

T he leek has to be king of the winter vegetables. It is the easiest of the onion family to grow. It will tolerate a range of winter conditions, from wet to very cold, and once mature it can be left in the ground for weeks while you harvest. You can extend the cropping period by choosing different varieties to mature at different times.

Varieties

'Bandit': A new variety that is described as outstanding for the garden. It has lovely dark green leaves and pure white stems and has been shown to have good resistance to bolting and rust.

'Carlton': Another early variety producing good long white stems that are ready for harvesting in September right through to November. Has an RHS Award of Garden Merit.

'Musselburgh': A popular mid-season variety that produces shorter chunky stems.

'Oarsman F1': The stems bulk up quickly on this variety making it a good mid-season leek.

'Pancho': A very early maturing variety, but will still remain in good condition if left in the ground for the winter. Also has an RHS Award of Garden Merit.

'Toledo': A strong-growing reliable variety that can be harvested from November to late February.

Growing tips

Sowing and planting

Leeks like a sunny spot and a good fertile soil, so dig in plenty of garden compost or farmyard manure a few months in advance. A week or two before planting, sprinkle some fertiliser, such as Growmore, or chicken manure pellets over the soil.

Leeks can be sown in a seedbed on the plot, or in cell trays and pots. If sowing outdoors, prepare a small area of ground and dig and rake to a nice crumbly surface. Make a groove (drill) in the soil about 2.5cm/1in deep and

Fact file

- Germination can take 14–18 days.
- Wide-girth varieties are grown in raised beds and can reach up to 4kg/9lb in weight.
- Roots help break up clay soils.
- Earthing up creates the white stem.

water the bottom. Sow the leek seed thinly along the row, about 1cm/½in apart. Cover with soil and, when the seedlings are through, remove every other one to leave 2cm/¾in between each seedling. When these have reached nearly pencil thickness, they can be carefully lifted and planted out where they are to grow and be harvested.

If starting the leeks off in cell trays, fill with some multi-purpose compost and sow one seed per cell. When they are pencil size, they will be ready for planting out.

Before planting out leeks, soak the soil the day before if possible. Then put out a line of string and make 15cm/6in deep holes with a trowel or dibber along the row at 15cm/6in apart. If planting more than one row make these 30cm/12in apart.

Drop a leek plant into each hole and then pour in a generous amount of water, which will settle the soil around the roots. Don't fill in the hole with more soil, just leave the plant as it is.

Growing on

Keep the leeks well watered. If the young plants are allowed to dry out, it may induce bolting. Once they have become established, you can earth up the stems a little. Simply rake up the soil around the base of the stems to help blanch them (produce a longer white shank).

A general-purpose feed applied when you water the leeks will help bulk up the stems, but stop feeding by about August. Leeks are prone to a disease called rust, which as its name suggests looks like little flecks of gingery rust on the leaves. It is not something you can control but, fortunately, it is something that most leeks grow through and is not too detrimental to the crop.

WARM SALAD OF BABY LEEKS

This is an ideal recipe for baby leeks. If your leeks are already fairly large, use only the white part for this simple, delicious dish, which makes a great starter or light lunch.

Per person:
3–4 baby leeks
½ yolk of hard-boiled egg
1½ tbsp olive oil
1 tsp lemon juice
pinch of caster sugar
salt and freshly ground black pepper

1 Wash and steam the leeks for about 6 minutes, or longer if using larger ones.
2 Rub the yolk(s) through a nylon sieve to make very fine crumbs.
3 Combine the remaining ingredients to make the dressing.
4 Arrange the leeks on individual serving plates, pour over the dressing, sprinkle on the egg and serve immediately.

Calendar

- If you want to grow leeks for exhibiting in the autumn shows, they will need to be sown as early as Jan/Feb in trays in a greenhouse with a little heat.
- Leek moth can be damaging.

	JAN	FEB	MAR	APR	MAY	JUN	JUL	AUG	SEP	OCT	NOV	DEC
Sowing/ planting time	🌱	🌱										
Harvest time												

Container growing

Leeks are not usually suitable for container growing. However, there are a growing number of varieties, which have been bred for use as baby leeks. These will grow and mature to the size of ordinary leeks if left, but offer a tasty treat if eaten while still small – from about the thickness of a pencil.

Look out for varieties such as 'Atal' and 'Amor', also certain standard varieties such as 'King Richard'. Sown more thickly than traditional varieties, they can be harvested in as little as six to 12 weeks from sowing.

In the kitchen

Leeks are a versatile vegetable, being used as a milder alternative to onions in dishes or as a side dish in their own right. The beauty of this crop is that you don't get a glut at harvesting time, as they will remain in good condition in the soil for weeks, if not months, so you can lift as many or as few as you like.

Preparation and cooking: When preparing leeks, remove the outer leaves and cut off the bulk of the green leaves. Cut a long slit down from the top and place under a tap, peeling back the slit sections to clean out any dirt. Smaller, slender leeks are the best and the white base of the leek has the better flavour. Pick young, and enjoy the tender white stems baked or grilled whole, with a knob of butter or full-flavoured cheese sauce. To liven up the sauce, you could add a blue cheese, such as Stilton, mustard or smoked white fish. Alternatively, leeks are simply delicious just shredded and tossed in a pan with some butter. The green, fibrous upper part should be used in longer, slow-cooked dishes, such as soups, stews and casseroles.

Storage and freezing: Lifted leeks will store for about five days in a refrigerator. If you lift them leaving plenty of soil on the roots, you can pack them into a hole in a corner of the plot, loosely covered with soil, where they will keep a bit longer than five days. This way, if the ground is hard with frost you will be able to lift them more easily.

You shouldn't need to freeze leeks because of their long cropping period, but it is possible. Remove the green tops, chop into small pieces and blanch for three minutes. Drain and dry the leeks before placing cold into plastic bags and into the freezer.

♥ *Antibacterial and antifungal properties; high in potassium, folate, vitamins A and C.*

CHEESE-BAKED LEEKS

Serves 4

4 medium leeks, washed and trimmed
25g/1oz butter
50g/2oz fresh soft cheese
1 small egg, beaten
4 tbsp plain yoghurt
4 tbsp freshly grated Parmesan cheese
salt and freshly ground black pepper
pinch of ground coriander
3–4 tbsp fresh breadcrumbs

1 Preheat oven to 160°C/325°F/gas 3/fan oven 145°C and butter a shallow ovenproof dish.
2 Bring the leeks to the boil in a pan and simmer until tender. Strain and cut lengthways, then across into pieces. Arrange in the dish.
3 In a bowl, mix together the butter and soft cheese. Now add the egg, yoghurt, half of the Parmesan cheese and seasonings. Mix lightly and spoon over the leeks.
4 Combine the remaining Parmesan with the breadcrumbs and sprinkle over the top. Bake for 20–30 minutes until bubbling and brown.

Lettuces

This has to be one of the most popular vegetables to grow in your garden, allotment or on the patio. It is fast maturing, the ultimate salad ingredient and can be grown in a relatively small area. Sown in succession, crops can be produced nearly all year round. The choice of varieties is endless and it is best to try several.

Varieties

There are several different types of lettuce. **Butterhead** types have soft leaves and quite an open head. **Crisphead** types, such as Iceberg, are very crunchy with tightly wrapped heads. **Looseleaf** varieties, on the other hand, have more open heads so the leaves can easily be removed a few at a time when you want them, while the plant is in the ground. **Cos** types (Romaine) form long, narrow dense heads of crunchy leaves.

Within these types are many varieties and most are suitable for sowing in succession from March to about August. There are a few that are quite hardy and can be sown in autumn or early spring. Examples include 'Arctic King' or 'All The Year Round' (Butterhead types). Seeds are sometimes sold as mixed leaves.

Growing tips

Sowing and planting

Lettuce can be sown directly into the ground, or in cell trays first. In cell trays, the seedlings are protected from the weather and slugs and can be sown in February or early March under cover for an early crop. Plant out when they reach about 5cm/2in high.

Growing on

If sowing outside, thin the seedlings as soon as they emerge so that they are 2.5cm/1in apart. Continue to thin as they grow: for the narrow Cos lettuce leave about 15cm/6in of space between each plant. Larger Butterhead or Crisphead types will require about 30cm/12in between them. The spacings are not critical but you will find that, when grown closer together, the lettuce will form smaller heads which you may prefer.

Keep the crop well watered at all times. If lettuce is 'stressed' at any time, due to lack of water, it will bolt by suddenly shooting upwards.

Fact file

- Lettuce is a fast maturing crop so, rather than sow one long row and end up with a glut of lettuce, sow short rows at fortnightly intervals to give a succession of cropping.
- Try to water lettuce in the morning, or during the day if it is not too hot. Evening watering can increase the risk of disease.
- Grow mixtures of different varieties to provide a more interesting salad.

In the kitchen

Crisp, refreshing Cos or a bowl of fresh, mixed lettuce leaves sit well with almost every dish.

Preparation and cooking: Lettuce is easy to prepare, simply wash the leaves to remove any grit or insects. Slice thin sections through the Crisphead and Cos lettuce to produce narrow strips, which are easier to manage in a salad.

A large bowl of green leaves requires only a little, light dressing: drizzle a little olive oil, coat the leaves until glossy and finish with a splash of balsamic vinegar or lemon juice. Leaves combined with other ingredients and served as a main course can withstand more robust and flavoursome dressings. Diced shallots, capers, citrus zest and mustard will liven up a salad.

In some European countries, they cook lettuce, braising it with onions and other vegetables. The leaves can also be used to wrap other ingredients, and lettuce can make a delicious soup.

Storage: Lettuce will keep for three to five days in the fridge. It is not suitable for freezing.

♥ *Rich source of vitamins K and A with some vitamin C and many trace elements. Different varieties and colours of lettuce provide varying nutrient levels.*

Container growing

Lettuce is ideal for growing in containers, especially the Looseleaf types with leaves that can be harvested when you require them. Cos are also good because they are narrow and you will get more plants in a small area. You could plant them in growbags, which is cheaper than filling a large pot or trough with compost. Cut a large panel out of the growbag and then sow two rows of lettuce, or three if you are happy with smaller heads. After the seeds have germinated, thin the seedlings to 5cm/2in apart and allow to grow on, keeping the compost moist at all times. Harvest alternate lettuces when large enough, allowing the others to grow on.

CHINESE PORK IN LETTUCE PARCELS

Serves 2 as main dish or 4 as a starter

200g/7oz pork or chicken, diced
1 egg, beaten
1 tbsp soy sauce
2 tsp cornflour
1 'Little Gem' lettuce, washed and dried
1 tbsp dry sherry
120ml/4fl oz chicken stock
2 tbsp vegetable oil
2–3 mushrooms, finely chopped
200g/7oz bamboo shoots, finely chopped
pinch of salt

1. Combine the meat pieces in a bowl with the egg, soy sauce and 1 tsp of the cornflour and place in the fridge.
2. Remove the larger leaves from the lettuce and place on a dish in the fridge.
3. Combine the sherry, stock and cornflour.
4. Heat the oil in a wok or frying pan and stir-fry the meat mixture for 5–6 minutes.
5. Add the mushrooms and bamboo shoots to the pan and cook for another 3–4 minutes, stirring.
6. Add the stock mixture and simmer, stirring, until the meat is tender.
7. Place the meat mixture in a serving dish to take to the table, along with the plate of lettuce leaves. To serve, let each person take a lettuce leaf and fill with some of the meat mixture, roll up and enjoy!

Serve with: Cherry tomatoes

Calendar

- Sow some varieties as late as Oct under cloches. Lettuce can be grown through winter in a heated environment.
- Sow Mar–Oct.
- Harvest Apr–Dec.

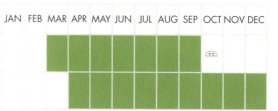

	JAN	FEB	MAR	APR	MAY	JUN	JUL	AUG	SEP	OCT	NOV	DEC
Sowing/ planting time			■	■	■	■	■	■	■	🔖		
Harvest time				■	■	■	■	■	■	■	■	■

Onions & shallots

Onions and shallots both belong to the Allium family but, whereas onions form one large bulb, shallots develop many small bulbs and are generally milder and sweeter – and ideal if you only cook for one or two people. Both are easy to grow in the garden, and perfect for planting among flowers if there is no room for a vegetable plot.

Varieties

ONIONS
'Ailsa Craig': An old favourite that produces large bulbs. Great for showing, too.
'Hi Keeper': A good variety to sow in late summer early autumn for overwintering as very hardy.
'New Fen Globe': Produces good large bulbs from early plantings.
'Red Baron': Superb red variety with beautiful mild flavour.
'Turbo': A good globe-shaped onion. Slow to bolt.

SHALLOTS
'Mikor': Round shallots with slightly pink flesh. Eight to ten bulbs per clump when mature in August.
'Pikant': A good early variety that stores well.

Growing tips

Sowing and planting
Prepare the soil well, digging it over and raking. Scatter some fertiliser, such as Growmore, or chicken manure pellets over it a week or two before sowing. Rake over again and firm by tamping down with the rake and gently rake over again.

Depending on the condition of your soil, you can sow as early as February but for most places in the UK especially after a wet winter, it will be mid-March, or April in Scotland, before conditions are favourable.

Onion seed: Sow seed fairly thickly along a drill about 1cm/½in deep. Once the seedlings are through, remove some to leave about 2.5–5cm/1–2in between them. When they are larger and more upright, thin them out again to about 10cm/4in apart. Remove the thinnings as the smell could encourage onion fly. The larvae will burrow into the base of the bulbs.

Onion sets: Plant the small onion sets 10cm/4in apart in rows 23cm/9in apart with the tips just showing above the surface of the soil.

Shallot sets: Plant these about 15cm/6in apart with the pointed tip just showing above the soil.

Fact file

- Spring onions can be sown at closer spacings as they are harvested small. Start sowing from March at intervals through the summer for a succession of crops.
- If onions are put under stress by being too dry at the roots, they may bolt. If this happens, cut off the flower heads and use the bulbs straight away, as they won't store well.

Growing on

Once the bulbs are growing well, keep the rows free of weeds. Weed by hand if possible as bulbs can be easily damaged by a wayward hoe. Water them if the weather is exceptionally dry, otherwise avoid it.

When the bulbs start to mature, the tops begin to yellow and eventually topple over. After this happens and during settled weather lift the bulbs leaving them on the surface for a couple of days to dry.

The bulbs can then be stored in a dry shed or garage in net bags or seed trays or tied into ropes.

Container growing

Shallots and onions are not an ideal crop for cultivating in containers, as you won't get a large harvest from a pot. However, a large enough pot or trough could provide a small crop. If you sow shallots rather than use sets, you may get a larger harvest of tiny bulbs, which may be more useful in the kitchen. Spring onions are an obvious choice for growing in a pot as they are harvested small. Use a John Innes No. 3 compost.

In the kitchen

Onions are our winter saviours; they store well and can be relied upon to add pungency, sweetness and depth to dishes throughout the year. Sulphur compounds within cells, which are released when the onion is cut and exposed to the air, cause the vapour that makes your eyes water. Once cut, onions and shallots rapidly loose their bite and flavour. Cut as required, or store in an airtight container.

Preparation and cooking: Onions and shallots can be used in so many different ways either raw or cooked, on their own as a dish or used with other ingredients. Used raw in salads is popular but, to temper the strength of the onions, pour boiling water over the chopped or sliced onions and dab them dry with kitchen paper. To maximise sweetness, cook them slowly over a low heat for a long time. This releases the natural sugars and starch, which begin to caramelise. Turning up the heat causes them to catch, becoming scorched and bitter. They are delicious roasted whole in their papery skins, or sliced, tossed and fried with plenty of butter and thyme.

Storage and freezing: Onions started off in spring and harvested in late summer will store for several months but the overwintering Japanese varieties will not store well and should be used as soon as possible. Shallots will keep for about eight months.

Onions store so well that freezing is not really necessary but it can be done if the onions are blanched for a minute or two before cooling and sealing in bags.

♥ *Good source of vitamins B and C. Red onions are high in the antioxidant anthocyanin.*

Calendar

- Sow large onions in Jan in pots or with some heat. Plant out in Apr.
- Sow onions Mar–Apr to harvest Aug–Sep.
- Sow onions Jul–early Sep to harvest Jul.
- Plant shallot or onion sets in Feb–Mar to harvest Jul.

■ = onions ▢ = shallots

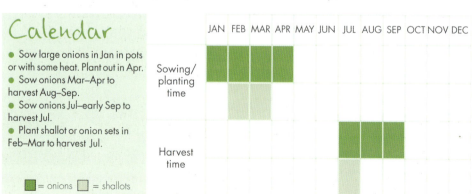

	JAN	FEB	MAR	APR	MAY	JUN	JUL	AUG	SEP	OCT	NOV	DEC
Sowing/ planting time	■	■	■	■								
		▢	▢									
Harvest time							■	■	■			
							▢					

ONION UPSIDE DOWN TART

This recipe makes the most of the versatile onion and offers a good way to make use of a bumper harvest.

Serves 4

1 tbsp olive oil
15g/½oz butter
2 large onions, sliced
3 garlic cloves, peeled and chopped
1 tsp sugar
1 tbsp balsamic vinegar
400g/14oz ready-made puff pastry
salt and freshly ground pepper

1 Preheat the oven to 200°C/400°F/gas 6/ fan oven 180°C. Heat the oil and butter in an ovenproof frying pan about 15cm/9in in diameter and stir in the onions and garlic. Cover and cook slowly for 10–12 minutes, stirring occasionally.
2 Add the sugar and vinegar and simmer uncovered for 5 minutes, or until the mixture starts to caramelise.
3 Roll out the pastry on a floured surface to the same size as the pan. Flatten the onions and cover with the pastry, pressing down gently around the sides.
4 Place in the oven, uncovered, and cook for 20–30 minutes until the pastry rises and appears to be cooked.
5 Remove from the oven and cool for 5 minutes, bearing in mind that the frying pan handle will stay hot for some time. Place a serving plate over the pan and invert, so that the tart sits pastry-side down on the plate. Serve hot or cold on its own, as a starter, or as part of a main course.

STUFFED ONIONS

Serves 2

2 medium-to-large onions, peeled
1 tbsp couscous or freshly cooked rice
2 tbsp boiling water
1 slice ham, chopped
25g/1oz Cheddar cheese or similar, grated
1 tomato, peeled and chopped
salt and freshly ground pepper
25g/1oz butter
1 tsp brown sugar

1 Preheat the oven to 180°C/350°F/gas 4/fan oven 160°C. Parboil the onions in a pan for about 10 minutes. Lift out the onions when they are soft enough for you to remove the centres while keeping the outer layers intact. Put the centres to one side and keep the cooking water.
2 Meanwhile, soak the couscous in the 2 tbsp of boiling water. After the water has been soaked up, mix in the ham, cheese and tomato. Chop one of the onion centres you put to one side, add it to the couscous mixture and season. If using freshly cooked rice, there is no need to soak it in the water.
3 Stuff the mixture into the centre of both onion shells, keeping their shape, and place in a small ovenproof casserole. Divide the butter and add half to the top of each onion then sprinkle with sugar. Pour 2 tbsp of the cooking water around them, cover and bake in the oven for 10 minutes to brown the top. You can save any leftover cooking water and onion centre to form the basis of a soup.

Parsnips

This delicious winter vegetable is not difficult to grow once it gets established. However, it does need a large plot because it is sown in March and not harvested until at least November and you need a large enough area to have a good-sized crop of roots, although you can sow quicker maturing crops between the rows.

Varieties

'Avon resister': Can be grown close together at about 7cm/3in apart. Has good canker resistance.

'Dagger F1': Has an Award of Garden Merit from the RHS. Smooth roots and good canker resistance – ideal for mini roots.

'Gladiator F1': A hybrid parsnip which means it should produce more uniform plants and roots of excellent quality. Has a lovely smooth, white skin and a very sweet flavour. Ideal for exhibition purposes.

'Javelin F1': Another variety that can be harvested for mini or full-grown roots.

'Tender and True': A popular variety that is good for the kitchen and for exhibiting. Also has good canker resistance.

'White Gem': Heavy yields and canker resistant.

Growing tips

Sowing and planting

Prepare the soil well by digging it over deeply to break up any hard layers and remove any large stones. There is no need to add manure or heavily feed the ground where parsnips are to grow.

The soil should be raked over well to form a fine tilth or crumbly surface. Put out a line and make a shallow seed drill along it. Water the bottom of the drill well and then sow. Parsnip seed is quite large and easy to handle. Either sow quite thickly along the row or two or three seeds every couple of inches.

Fact file

- Seed germination is erratic and can take 2–3 weeks.
- Always buy fresh seed each year, as it does not store well.
- If seed germination is poor try sowing some on wet kitchen paper first and then gently sow the seeds when the root emerges.
- Canker disease can cause problems leading to a black rotted area around the top of the root. Modern varieties have good resistance.

Growing on

As the parsnips grow, thin out the plants until you have about 15cm/6in between them. This will leave room for each root to develop. Remove weeds regularly and water the crop in dry spells to achieve good-sized roots by early winter.

In the kitchen

In the cold winter months this often ignored vegetable can add a subtle sweetness to the most basic winter food. A good frost while the roots are in the ground converts some of the starch into sugar, making them sweeter and more tasty.

Preparation and cooking: Even small, young parsnips can have a tough, indigestible core. If dark or woody, remove the centre. A popular way to eat parsnips is sliced and roasted until crisp. A sprinkling of rosemary adds a tasty twist. Combine with other root vegetables, such as swede, celeriac or potatoes, for a dish of roast vegetables and in thick, filling soups and stews, or to create an interesting mash. Parboiled, then roasted with honey is a Christmas classic.

Storage and freezing: Parsnips are best left in the ground and lifted when wanted but will keep for a couple of weeks in the fridge. To freeze, they should be washed, peeled and cut into chunks and then blanched for five minutes before putting in freezer bags.

♥ *High in vitamin C, folate, potassium and fibre.*

The parsnips are ready for lifting once the foliage has died down which will be late autumn or the beginning of winter. The roots won't put on any more growth at this stage, so you can dig them up as and when required – they will happily sit in the ground all winter. It is said that the sweetest flavoured parsnips are those that have experienced a frost or two.

Container growing

Parsnips are not the ideal vegetable for container growing. They need good deep soil and, having large leafy tops, you won't get too many in a pot. However, if you have a large trough, at least 60cm/2ft deep and with a good length and reasonable drainage, you could grow one of the mini varieties such as 'Dagger F1'.

Calendar

- Sow Mar–early Apr.
- Sow mini roots Mar–end May.
- Use parsnips before they begin to regrow in late winter or lift and store in boxes of moist sand for a month.

	JAN	FEB	MAR	APR	MAY	JUN	JUL	AUG	SEP	OCT	NOV	DEC
Sowing/ planting time			▓	▓	▓							
Harvest time											▓	▓

FRUITY PARSNIPS

Serves 2

4 medium parsnips (about 350g/12oz), peeled and diced
1 tbsp sunflower oil
1 tbsp orange marmalade
1 onion, finely chopped
1 cooking apple, peeled and finely chopped
salt and freshly ground pepper

1 Boil the parsnips in a large pan for 5 minutes, then strain.
2 Warm the oil in another pan and stir in the marmalade. Add the parsnip, onion and apple and turn well to coat in oil.
3 Turn the heat up to medium and cook covered for 5 minutes until the contents are soft but not browned. Stir in a little water if the mixture starts to get too sticky.
4 Add salt and pepper to taste. Turn off the heat and allow to rest for 5 minutes before serving.

CINNAMON SPICED PARSNIPS

Here's a winter warmer and a great way to ring the changes with those sweet, frosted parsnips.

Serves 4

450g/1lb parsnips, peeled
flour, seasoned with salt and freshly ground pepper
50g/2oz butter
½ tsp ground cinnamon
chopped fresh parsley to garnish

1 Slice the parsnips into 5mm/¼in slices. Roll in the seasoned flour. Heat the butter in a pan, stirring in the cinnamon.
2 Once the butter starts to sizzle, drop in the parsnips and fry until golden.
3 Garnish with fresh, chopped parsley.

Peas

Peas are packed with nutrients, especially when picked straight from the garden when they have a really superior taste. Even better value to grow are the sugar snap and mangetout varieties, which you eat pod and all. Always dig pea roots back into the ground as they contain nitrogen-fixing nodules on their roots that benefit the soil.

Varieties

'Alderman': A late maincrop variety that grows to about 1.5m/5ft high.
'Delikett': A very sweet sugar snap variety growing to about 75cm/30in. An RHS Award of Merit winner.
'Early Onward': A very heavy cropping variety that also benefits from early sowings.
'Feltham First': A popular dwarf variety that is particularly good for sowing very early or late in the season. Doesn't need much supporting.
'Greensage': Bred from the popular 'Greenshaft' variety but said to be even sweeter.
'Pea Oregon': An RHS Award of Merit winner, this mangetout plant grows to about 100cm/3¼ft high.

Growing tips

Sowing and planting

Peas can be sown directly into the ground from March. Sow seeds about 5cm/2in apart in a single or double row and to a depth of 4cm/1½in. However, the seeds are very attractive to birds and mice, so cover them with netting or sow under cover in pots or trays in a cold frame or greenhouse.

Another method is sowing into a piece of guttering filled with compost. Once the seedlings are through, the compost can be gently pushed out of the guttering straight into a prepared shallow trench.

Fact file

- Pea seeds can be wrinkled or smooth. Round pea varieties tend to be harder and are more suited to very early sowings.
- Mangetout or snow peas are grown for their flat pods that are picked when young and eaten whole.
- Sugar snap peas are a stage on from the mangetout and can be picked and eaten whole when their pods have started to swell.
- Petit pois, such as the variety 'Waverex', produce pods with numerous small peas.

Growing on

Some pea varieties are short while other, often older, varieties will grow up to 1.5m/5ft or more. All have quite spindly stems so will need support. The dwarf ones can be supported using twigs stuck in the ground among the crop. Taller varieties will require netting. Twine stems around the supports if necessary.

Once the crop starts to flower and the pods form, keep the plants well watered.

A white coating on the leaves indicates mildew. Prune out and destroy affected leaves. Make sure plants are well spaced, mulch the ground and use an all-purpose rather than nitrogen-rich feed.

SPINACH PEAS

Serves 4

2 tbsp vegetable oil
1 medium onion, finely chopped
small piece of root ginger, peeled
250ml/8fl oz vegetable stock
1 tsp sugar
225g/8oz fresh shelled peas
handfuls of small spinach leaves (or outer leaves of a mature lettuce)
balsamic vinegar or fruit vinegar (optional)

1 Heat the oil in a pan and cook the onion gently until softened with the ginger. Add the stock and sugar, turn the heat to medium and pour in the peas, cover and simmer for 2–3 minutes.
2 When the peas are almost ready, stir in the spinach or lettuce and continue to simmer until soft.
3 Serve in bowls, removing the ginger first. There should be enough stock left to spoon over each serving. Add a shake of vinegar if desired.

In the kitchen

Home-grown peas rarely make it as far as the kitchen. They are so delicious eaten straight from the pod and at this point contain the most nutrients. However, if you grow a lot of peas, you will want to harvest some for cooking later. These little green gems add colour and sweetness to an array of dishes.

Preparation and cooking: Podding peas can be a laborious, but worthwhile chore. Have a couple of bowls ready and get everyone involved! Or choose mangetout or sugar snap and avoid the job altogether! Compost the pods. Peas are spoiled by overcooking; eat raw or cook for a few minutes in boiling water or soften in hot butter. Don't add salt during cooking, it makes the skins tough and taut. They are delicious with lush soft parsley, mint and lashings of butter! Also good cooked with diced shallots, cream and fresh mint and crushed into a vivid green purée, ideal with fish or lamb.

Storage and freezing: Peas are best picked and eaten straight away, they will lose nutrients as they age. The pods will keep for two days in the fridge.

Peas are the perfect vegetable for freezing; it is the best way of preserving them as they will retain their goodness if you open-freeze them on trays quickly after harvesting.

♥ High in vitamin C.

Container growing

Peas can be grown in containers, especially the shorter varieties. They may still need some sticks to support them. You could also grow the perfect container pea called 'Half Pint' which reaches about 30–38cm/12–15 in tall. It is so small you could plant five seeds in a 15cm/6in diameter pot and still get a little harvest, at least a taster! It dates back to the 1800s and is said to be very tolerant of the cold – down to –6°C/20°F. It's a good variety to grow in a cold frame or even in a pot on the windowsill.

Calendar

● Sow in autumn in pots or seed or cell trays in a cold frame or greenhouse.
● Sow into well-drained soil in the plot in Mar in milder areas. Cover with cloches in severe weather.

	JAN	FEB	MAR	APR	MAY	JUN	JUL	AUG	SEP	OCT	NOV	DEC
Sowing/ planting time			■	■	■	■			🐛	🐛	🐛	
Harvest time					■	■	■	■				

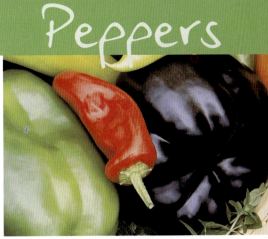

Peppers

There are two types of pepper, or capsicum: chilli peppers and sweet peppers. Peppers are not the easiest of crops to grow because they need warmth and sun, but given the right conditions they will produce a good harvest. Ideally grow peppers in a greenhouse or polytunnel, or look out for varieties that will do well in pots on a patio.

Varieties

SWEET PEPPERS

'Tasty Grill Red F1': Produces long red fruits up to 25cm/10in in length. They are delicious sliced and grilled or stuffed, or used in salads. Said not to 'repeat' on eating which is what puts some people off peppers! There is also a yellow form, 'Tasty Grill Yellow F1'.

'Big Banana F1': Really sweet fruits up to 25cm/10in long. They mature to a bright red.

'Gypsy F1': Masses of fruits up to 10cm/4in long and 8cm/3in wide that turn orange to red. Crops earlier than some varieties.

CHILLI PEPPERS

'Jalapeno Summer Heat F1': This is the pizza pepper! It has long narrow fruits that can be picked when green or left to mature to red.

'Numex Twilight': An attractive small plant to grow in a pot on the patio. The masses of tiny fruits ripen from purple to yellow, orange and red and all these colours can be on the plant at once.

'Thai Dragon F1': A truly hot variety that is a prolific cropper of 9cm/3½in red fruits.

Growing tips

Sowing and planting

Peppers need a long growing season, so are usually sown quite early in February or March. Sow several seeds in small pots of multi-purpose compost. Water well and place in a propagator or airing cupboard. They need temperatures of about 15–21°C/60–70°F to germinate.

Once the seedlings are large enough to handle, transplant them, one seedling per small 9cm/3½in pot. Place on a warm sunny windowsill to grow on.

They may need to be moved on to the next pot size before planting out, but by about mid April to early May they can be transferred to the greenhouse and be planted in large 13cm/5in pots or growbags.

Peppers which are going to be grown on a patio will need to be kept indoors for longer. On warm, sunny days they can be placed outside but brought in at night. By the beginning of June, they can be planted into their final pots out on the patio.

Growing on

Some of the dwarf peppers will naturally form more bushy plants. The taller growing ones should be given a cane support and tied in at regular intervals. Keep the plants well watered but be careful not to overwater. It can take some time for the peppers to change colour – anything up to three weeks.

Fact file

● Can take 2–3 weeks to germinate.
● Some peppers (chilli) are perennial so can be kept over winter if warm enough and brought into growth the following spring.
● Capsaicin is the ingredient that makes chillis hot and this is beneficial to our health. In countries where chillies are eaten regularly, deaths from cancer are much lower than in countries where pepper consumption is low. It is thought capsaicin inhibits cancer cells. It has also been found to give pain relief to arthritic joints in cream form.

Container growing

A perfect plant to grow in containers. If growing in a greenhouse, they will do very well in large pots or growbags. Plant three peppers per growbag. They would also look spectacular grown in large 30cm/12in diameter pots placed on a sunny patio. Put three plants in this size pot for a really bushy effect. Try using 'Numex Twylight', which is very attractive and easy to grow.

In the kitchen

Use glossy sweet peppers to add summer sweetness and colour to your plate. Green varieties are the sharpest and most acidic, followed by yellow, orange and red, which are deliciously sweet. Chilli peppers are for the tougher tastebuds and need to be used sparingly but they certainly are far superior used fresh than processed in powdered form.

Preparation and cooking: Cut away the stalk, seeds and white membrane of sweet peppers. The skin too is sometimes peeled as it's tough and does not break down during cooking. Or rub with oil and place under a hot grill until blistered, then peel off the skin under the tap. Rub your hands with oil before preparing chilli and do not touch eyes or lips as the juice will sting.

Peppers have many uses in the kitchen. Sweet peppers add a bit of colour to green salads, sliced into rings. They are wonderful roasted, removing the skins after roasting.

These soft, sweet, roasted peppers can be sliced and tossed through pastas, salads and sauces. Their bulbous shape and size makes them ideal for stuffing and baking: any combination of rice, creamy cheeses and fresh herbs, or mince, is perfect.

Storage and freezing: Peppers will store for a couple of weeks in the fridge, but they do not freeze well.

♥ *Good source of vitamins B, K and A, and iron. Green peppers provide carotenoids, known to help reduce age-related eye disorders; orange peppers contain important vitamins that may help prevent lung problems; red peppers contain lycopene, which can help reduce risk of prostate and some other cancers.*

CHILLI PRAWN SALAD

If you prefer only a hint of chilli, just drop the two halves into the oil rather than chopping it up first . If you enjoy a bit of heat, sprinkle the salad with some tiny chopped pieces.

Serves 2

5 tbsp olive oil
1 small chilli, halved and finely chopped
225g/8oz shelled prawns
lettuce or rocket leaves
2 medium courgettes, 1 yellow and 1 green
juice of ½ lemon
small handful of fresh parsley, chopped
salt and freshly ground pepper

1 Place the oil in a bowl. Add chilli and prawns and leave for a couple of hours.
2 Arrange lettuce or rocket leaves on plates. Cut the courgettes into thin strips with a vegetable peeler. Arrange on top of the lettuce.
3 Take prawns from their marinade and arrange on top of the courgettes. Mix the lemon juice into the remaining chilli oil and sprinkle over the dish.
4 Sprinkle with parsley and season with salt and pepper.

Calendar

● Sow Feb–Mar in propagator, put in greenhouse end Apr–early May, harvest Jul–Oct.
● For outdoor growing, sow under cover in Mar, put out in Jun and harvest Aug–Oct.

	JAN	FEB	MAR	APR	MAY	JUN	JUL	AUG	SEP	OCT	NOV	DEC
Sowing/ planting time		☂	☂	☂	☂	■						
Harvest time							■	■	■	■		

With such a constant supply of cheap potatoes in our supermarkets why should you bother to grow your own? For the pleasure of lifting your own first early spuds, of course! Nothing beats that taste of your first home-grown potatoes boiled with a sprig of mint and served with a knob of butter.

Varieties

There are so many varieties that can be planted throughout the growing season. The following are popular varieties or new ones that have extremely good disease resistance.

FIRST EARLIES

'Arran Pilot': A very popular early potato with a fantastic new potato flavour.

'Epicure': A good white potato with creamy flesh. Best one to recover if touched by frost.

Second earlies

'British Queen': More than 100 years old, this variety produces good harvests of floury potatoes that have a delicious flavour.

'Estima': A heavy cropper. Drought resistant and produces good baking potatoes.

EARLY MAINCROP

'Desiree': Probably the most popular red variety. Great all rounder and heavy cropper.

'Sante': A good potato for pest and disease resistance.

'Belle de Fontenay': A popular variety with chefs because of its wonderful flavour.

'Smile': Aptly named as this red potato has white smile shaped markings. Great flavour as bred from red 'Duke of York'.

LATE MAINCROP

'Cara': A good drought and disease resistant variety that makes a great baking potato.

'Pink Fir Apple': A red knobbly shaped salad potato renowned for its delicious flavour. The shape makes them trickier to peel but the flavour is worth it.

'Sarpo Mira': A new variety that has proven to have really good blight resistance. Not attractive to slugs.

Growing tips

Sowing and planting

Potatoes grow from tubers, which are the storage organs produced by the roots. They are planted in spring and shoots and new roots form from this tuber, producing more tubers. From early summer, depending on the variety, they can be lifted and the new tubers harvested.

   Seed potatoes are usually available in garden centres from about January when they

Fact file

- If potato tubers are exposed to the light they turn green, which is poisonous. To avoid this, draw soil up the stems as much as possible.
- After lifting potatoes, the leaves and stems can be put on the compost heap.
- If potato flowers are pollinated small fruits are produced that look like green tomatoes – potatoes and tomatoes are related. But these fruits are poisonous – the potato is also in the same family as the deadly nightshade.

should be chitted. This means placing the tubers in a tray with the 'eyes' (buds) facing upwards to encourage them to shoot. Put the trays in a light, frost-free spot such as near a window in a shed or garage.

Plant the potatoes about 13cm/5in deep and 30cm/12in apart with the chitted shoots facing upwards. Maincrop potatoes tend to be in the ground longer and produce larger plants, so plant these about 38cm/15in apart. Rows should be about 60cm/2ft apart for earlies and 75cm/30in apart for maincrop varieties.

Growing on

Once the leaves appear above the soil surface, cover them with soil. This has two purposes: it protects the leaves from frost and it also helps elongate the stems which will encourage more roots and tubers to form. This process is called earthing up and is best done two or three times as the plants grow. If potatoes do get frosted they may turn black. Sometimes they will grow through this damage, but it is best to avoid it in the first place.

When the plants start to produce flower buds, it is most important they are given adequate moisture because the tubers will be small and starting to swell. Drought at this time will result in very small potatoes.

During flowering, scrape away a little soil to see if the tubers are large enough to lift. New potatoes should be harvested quite small, about the size of a hen's egg.

Weeks to harvesting are: first earlies 20, second earlies 13, early maincrops 15, late maincrops 20.

In the kitchen

Contrary to popular belief, potatoes are good for you but only as long as they are not coated in fat or covered in butter! They are packed with vitamins and carbohydrates. The skins are very nutritious too, so resist peeling.

Preparation and cooking: New potatoes are the easiest to prepare as they only need washing, although some people like to rub off the skins. These first earlies are best eaten simply boiled with mint and served with butter and fresh chopped parsley. Older potatoes have many uses. Some varieties are better for baking, chips or mash. A good example is 'Golden Wonder', well known for its chipping and crisp-making qualities.

For the cook, apart from the flavour, there is just one important distinction to be made between types of potato – whether it is waxy or floury. Waxy potatoes have a higher sugar content and firm texture. They are sweet, moist and will not absorb water and crumble during cooking. Ideal for use in salads or anywhere you wish your spud to keep its shape and bite. Floury potatoes are usually late season and have a dry crumbly texture due to the sugars converting into starch. They absorb water and break down when boiled. Perfect for mashing, but also frying – the drier the potato, the crisper it will become.

Storage and freezing: Store in a cool, dark and dry place; do not refrigerate. Scrub and peel as required, they will become dry and discoloured if left exposed too long. The first early varieties do not store well and are best eaten as soon as possible. The best storers are the maincrop varieties. These can be lifted when large enough, preferably on a dry, sunny day and left on the surface for an hour or two. Don't leave any longer or they will be in danger of turning green. Once dry, store in hessian or paper sacks. Any damaged potatoes must be put to one side and eaten as soon as possible. Only the perfect potatoes will store for several months. Tie up the sack and place in a cool, dark spot in a garage or shed.

❤ High in vitamins C, B6 and B1, folate and potassium; the skin is high in fibre.

Calendar

- Plant first earlies early Mar–mid May.
- Plant second earlies or early maincrop Mar–late May.
- Plant late maincrop end Mar–late May.

	JAN	FEB	MAR	APR	MAY	JUN	JUL	AUG	SEP	OCT	NOV	DEC
Sowing/ planting time			■	■	■							
Harvest time						■	■	■	■			

BUBBLE AND SQUEAK

This dish is said to have originated from the initial bubbling of vegetables in the pan when first cooked, followed by the squeaking as they were later fried. An old favourite – served with plump juicy sausages, lamb chops or freshly cut cold ham – it can be found on menus around the UK. Perfect for using left-over vegetables. If cooking the vegetables fresh, allow them to go completely cold before trying to shape into cakes and they will be less likely to fall apart when fried.

Serves 4

450g/1lb floury potatoes, peeled and cut into chunks
225g/8oz swede, peeled and diced
50g/2oz butter
225g/8oz Brussels sprouts
salt and freshly ground black pepper
freshly grated nutmeg
vegetable oil for frying

1 In separate pans of lightly salted water cook the potatoes and swede for 15–20 minutes until tender. Drain, and then mash the potatoes with the butter. Lightly crush the swede with a fork.
2 Meanwhile, cook the sprouts for 6–8 minutes until tender. Drain and cool, then chop.
3 Mix all the vegetables together in a large bowl and season with the salt, pepper and nutmeg. Chill in the fridge for at least 30 minutes. Shape into 8 small cakes or 4 larger ones.
4 Heat the oil in a large frying pan and fry the cakes for about 15 minutes, turning once, until crispy and golden brown.

CHILLI HOT POTATOES

Serves 2

2 tbsp sunflower oil
2 large potatoes, peeled and thinly sliced
1 large onion, chopped
1 sweet green pepper, deseeded and diced
1 chilli pepper (use less or more to taste), deseeded and chopped

1 Heat the oil in a large frying pan or skillet and when hot add the potatoes and the onion.
2 Cook for 8–10 minutes turning regularly to prevent the mixture sticking. Stir in the green pepper during the last couple of minutes.
3 Top with the chilli pepper when the potatoes are cooked and just before serving, so that it remains quite crunchy. This dish can be made successfully with cold potatoes heated up for 4–5 minutes.

Container growing

Potatoes can be grown in containers and there are special potato barrels and bags available to buy. You can also plant them in a large bag of compost. Simply remove three quarters of the compost and put to one side. Fold back the sides of the bag and make some holes in the base for drainage. Plant three tubers in the few inches of compost at the bottom. This can be done as early as late February if you have a greenhouse or polytunnel.

As the potatoes grow, put back some of the compost to just cover the new shoots. Do this two to three times, gradually unrolling the bag. This will encourage elongated stems and more roots beneath the compost, which will produce more tubers. Keep the compost just moist, never soaking wet, and place outside in April or May but cover the foliage if a late frost is forecast. When the potatoes are flowering feel around in the compost to see if the tubers are big enough to lift. If not leave a little longer and keep well watered.

Radishes

'**French Breakfast 3':** A classic variety of long red and white roots, perfect for summer salads.
'**Zlata':** An unusual yellow variety with white flesh and oval roots. Ideal for mixing with red radish for great colour.

Growing tips

Sowing and planting
Radishes will tolerate a little shade and are ideal for planting between larger-leaved vegetables. They are usually sown directly where you want them to grow with about 2.5cm/1in between seeds in rows about 15cm/6in apart. Growing them close together helps to keep the radishes small and tender. Winter radishes are usually given more space, at least 15cm/6in between plants.

The young seedlings are particularly vulnerable to flea beetles, which punch tiny holes in the leaves. Prevent an attack by covering the plants with horticultural fleece.

Growing on
Water the crop well especially in drought conditions to encourage stronger, hardier roots. Harvest when the roots are about the size of a 10 pence piece; long, thin varieties should be left until they are about 13–17cm/5–7in long and winter varieties can be lifted when required.

Container growing
Radishes are perfect for growing in containers as they are small and can be sown close together. If you sow a 38cm/15in pot with plenty of seed, allowing overcrowding of seedlings, it will help restrict the size of the roots and you can harvest some tiny but delicious radishes for sandwiches and salads over a week or two.

Fast to mature and easy to grow, radishes can be grown between slower crops, such as leeks or brassicas, making good use of a small plot. There are winter varieties that are usually larger and some are black, which make a useful addition to the garden in the leaner months. They have a very strong flavour that softens when cooked.

Varieties

'**Cherry Belle':** This produces small round all-red roots, milder than some radish.
'**F1 Mantanghong':** Winter variety that has a red flesh and nutty flavour.

Fact file

- Germination can take as little as 4 days.
- Crops can be harvested in as little as 3 weeks after sowing.
- Seed remains viable for up to 6 years.

Calendar
- If sown Feb–early Mar, cover with cloches to protect them from the frost and cold winds.
- Water regularly in summer to avoid the roots splitting – a problem after heavy rain.

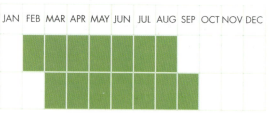

	JAN	FEB	MAR	APR	MAY	JUN	JUL	AUG	SEP	OCT	NOV	DEC
Sowing/ planting time		■	■	■	■	■	■	■				
Harvest time			■	■	■	■	■	■	■			

Runner beans

Runner beans must be the all-time favourite beans, although they can be a bit temperamental. This is often caused by hot weather which can stop the production of beans, but usually a drop in temperature will get them going again. They like a well-prepared soil with plenty of compost or manure. Strong supports are essential.

Varieties

'Enorma': A good runner bean to grow if you want long pods to exhibit in your local flower show.

'Painted Lady': A classic variety producing unusual bi-coloured red and white flowers. Attractive in the flower border.

'Sun Bright': Has gold-tinged leaves which contrast with its red flowers. Not as vigorous as many other varieties and later cropping.

'Sunset': A pretty, pale pink-flowered form that can be kept compact by removing the growing tips when it is still quite small.

Fact file

● Place a layer of grass cuttings along the inside of a double row of runner beans. It will help contain the moisture in the soil and keep weed growth down.

● Some gardeners dig a trench in autumn and put in their green kitchen scraps and grass clippings. By planting time, they will have rotted down enough to provide a rich planting base, which will retain a lot of water.

'White Lady': Has white flowers that are less attractive to birds. White-flowered varieties are believed to set better in higher temperatures.

Growing tips

Sowing and planting

Runner beans are sensitive to cold so if you want an early start in March or early April, sow into pots or cell trays and keep in the warm. Sow four beans to a 10cm/4in pot filled with a multi-purpose compost, or one seed per cell if using cell trays. Plant the seeds vertically about 5cm/2in deep, cover with compost, water well and place in a propagator or on a warm windowsill. It will take 7–14 days for the seedlings to emerge. Remove from the propagator as soon as the seedlings start to break through the surface of the soil. They will stretch and go leggy if left in the heat for too long. Place seedlings in a greenhouse or cold frame outside from about mid April.

Growing on

Choose a sunny spot to grow your beans and after incorporating some garden compost and a sprinkling of chicken manure or fertiliser, such as Growmore, erect a support frame. These can be two rows of 1.8m/6ft canes, crossed and tied at the top, or a wigwam effect of five or six canes. Position the canes about 30cm/12in apart.

By late May, or early June in colder areas of the country, the beans can be planted out. Tie the stem to the cane loosely to encourage the bean to grow up that support. Use slug control at this stage.

Water the plants in well and keep them well

In the kitchen

A prolific summer vegetable that provides nutrition and texture for the table, a good runner bean crop needs picking every day or you'll find a glut of large, tough pods. The beans' sugars will start turning to starch after picking, so they are best eaten as fresh as possible.

Preparation and cooking: The larger beans tend to need de-stringing, by cutting off the stringy-like fibre down each side of the pod, then slice diagonally along the bean. Young beans that are not too long can be left whole. They are best cooked quickly, on the soft side of al dente for maximum flavour. Sliced runner beans can be blanched, stir-fried or steamed and served smothered in butter, salt and freshly ground black pepper.

Storage and freezing: Store in a cool, dry place for a couple of days if necessary. To freeze, wash the beans and remove the stalk ends. De-string and slice. Blanch for two to three minutes and cool before sealing in plastic bags or boxes and freezing. They will keep for about 12 months.

♥ High in vitamins A, C and K, fibre and protein.

TARRAGON AND THREE-BEAN SALAD

This dish can be served hot as a side dish or cold as a salad.

Serves 4

700g/1½lb young runner beans and yellow and green French beans
2 tsp olive oil
3 ripe tomatoes, skinned and diced
sea salt and freshly ground black pepper
½ tsp dried oregano
2 tsp chopped tarragon
2 tsp chopped chives

1 Steam the beans whole until tender but they should still have a slight bite.
2 Heat the oil in a saucepan and cook the tomatoes until heated through.
3 Add the beans, salt, pepper and oregano and half the tarragon and chives. Toss well and just before serving sprinkle over the remaining herbs.

watered, especially when flowering starts, adding a general liquid feed once a week. Once the beans have reached a good length, start picking them – daily if possible to encourage the plants to keep producing flowers and set fruit.

When the plants have reached the top of their supports, remove the growing tips to prevent them growing any taller.

Container growing

If you have a large enough pot, you could grow runner beans up a wigwam of canes. Add some sweet peas too and you will have a very decorative planter for the patio. The problem with growing runner beans in a container is the danger of the soil drying out, which will stop the production of beans. A large container will hold enough soil to keep moist easily.

If you have a smaller container try growing the dwarf runner bean 'Hestia'. This only grows to about 30cm/12in and has red and white flowers. Grow several in a large pot for greatest impact and fruiting.

Calendar

● Sow in containers under cover Mar–Apr to protect against frosts and pests.
● Sow directly into the ground end Apr–Jun.
● Harvest Jun–Oct.

	JAN	FEB	MAR	APR	MAY	JUN	JUL	AUG	SEP	OCT	NOV	DEC
Sowing/ planting time			👓	👓	■	■						
Harvest time						■	■	■	■	■		

Salad leaves

The popularity of the expensive bags of salad leaves in supermarkets has motivated many to grow their own salad leaves. They are so cheap and easy to grow, and all you need is a windowbox or growbag. The choice of salad leaves is immense. They look great and taste wonderful and you can keep them coming all summer.

Varieties

American land cress, beetroot 'Bulls Blood', endive, green in the snow (perilla or shiso), komatsuna, lamb's lettuce, leaf beet, mibuna, mizuna, mustard, pak choi, radish leaf, red orach, rocket, salad burnet, senposai, spinach, tatsoi.

This list is not exhaustive; there are more available and some of those mentioned can be left to grow to maturity, such as pak choi and endive (see page 35), to provide a much meatier crop. The seedling leaves are ideal for tossing into a salad, too. Mustard is a popular salad leaf and there are many different types giving

different leaf shapes and colours and strength of taste. In the mixed seed collections there may be four or five of the above in one packet.

Growing tips

Sowing and planting

Sow salad leaves in short rows or in pots Simply sprinkle the seed fairly close together in the row. There is often no need to thin out the crop unless they were sown too thickly. If you do have to thin them out, use the thinnings in a salad.

Fact file

- Salad leaves can be mixed with herbs to create even more flavour. Use basil, thyme or mint.
- Look out for some interesting oils to sprinkle on salad leaves, which will provide even greater nutrition.

- Harvest leaves with scissors or just snap off individual leaves with your fingers.

Growing on

Keep the crop well watered and as soon as the leaves are 8–10cm/3–4in high, you can start picking them. Try not to take out the main growing tip but remove the young leaves at the sides.

Salad leaves are fast growing, which also means they are quick to 'go over' and get too large and coarse, or too strong in flavour. Rocket is prone to going to flower and seed very quickly, although you can eat the hot, peppery flowers, too.

For a continuous harvest of young leaves, you need to sow successionally. This means sowing a short row or a pot full of salad leaves every fortnight.

Container growing

Salad leaves are the perfect vegetable for growing in a container, especially some of the mixtures of salad leaves now available. They are quick to grow and in a matter of days you can be pinching a few leaves from a pot to add to a salad or a sandwich. Sow a growbag of mixed salad leaves and place by your kitchen door, making them really convenient.

Calendar

- Very early or late sowings in Feb or Nov will need cloches, a polytunnel or greenhouse.
- Sow Mar–Nov every 2 weeks for a constant supply of leaves.
- Harvest May–Mar.

	JAN	FEB	MAR	APR	MAY	JUN	JUL	AUG	SEP	OCT	NOV	DEC
Sowing/ planting time		🌱	■	■	■	■	■	■	■	■	🌱	
Harvest time	■	■	■		■	■	■	■	■	■	■	■

In the kitchen

Peppery rocket or spicy oriental leaves, a bowl of fresh, mixed salad leaves straight from the garden or pot, sits well with almost every dish.

Preparation and cooking: Salad leaves should be picked and used immediately. Wash in cold water before adding to lettuce or salad. A large bowl of green leaves in different colours and textures as an accompaniment only requires a little light dressing: coat the leaves with a drizzle of olive oil until glossy and finish with a splash of balsamic vinegar or lemon juice. Dress leaves just before serving or at the table. Coated too early they become limp and discoloured.

Some salad leaves are suited better to particular dishes: rocket with its peppery taste is delicious with cold meats, especially beef. Leaves combined with other ingredients and served as a main course can withstand more robust and flavoursome dressings. Diced shallots, capers, citrus zest and mustard will all liven up your salad.

Storage: There is no need to store salad leaves when growing your own, just pick when required and you won't get fresher than that.

♥ *Salad leaves are highly nutritious especially if you combine several types and eat immediately after picking. Each has their own level of minerals and vitamins. They are particularly high in vitamin C.*

BLUE CHEESE AND CRUNCH DRESSING

For each serving

2oz/50g blue cheese such as Danish blue
2 tsp lemon juice
sea salt and freshly ground black pepper
1 tbsp crème fraîche or soured cream
2 tbsp olive oil
salad leaves
handful of croûtons to garnish

1 Combine all the ingredients, except the croûtons, in a blender until smooth.
2 Sprinkle over the salad leaves and garnish with the croûtons.

Spinach

Spinach is a love-it-or-hate-it vegetable when cooked but the young leaves are popular raw in salads. It has a reputation for being high in iron, although it has no more than some other leafy or green vegetables. However, spinach is extremely nutritious and, as it is easy to grow nearly all year round, it is a good choice for the vegetable plot.

Varieties

Some varieties of spinach have round seeds, which are usually sown in spring to be harvested throughout the summer. Another hardier type, with prickly seeds, can be harvested into autumn and winter. There is also New Zealand spinach, which isn't a true spinach, but looks similar with smaller leaves. It is milder in flavour and is more tolerant of hot weather.

Perpetual spinach is actually a member of the beetroot family.

'Samish': A late-sowing variety for growing under cloches or in polytunnels. Harvest the young leaves.

'Sigmaleaf': A popular summer variety that is bolt resistant and quite hardy, too, so can be grown for autumn and winter harvesting.

'Tirza F1': Good resistance to downy mildew, a disease that can be a problem on spinach. Also more resistant to bolting.

'Triathlon F1': Best from spring and autumn sowings. Fast growing.

Growing tips

Sowing and planting

Sow the seeds about 2.5cm/1in deep and 2.5cm/1in apart. Once the seedlings are through, thin them out to 8–15cm/3–6in apart. Don't allow spinach seedlings to remain too close, as they will bolt.

Growing on

Keep the weeds down around the plants and water well in dry spells. Start to pick the leaves as soon as they are large enough. Leave the growing point intact so that more leaves will be produced.

Fact file

- Sow spinach in a partly shaded spot where it is cooler and the soil will dry out less quickly. It can also be shaded by taller crops.
- Summer varieties tend to be more tender and softer while winter-grown spinach is coarser and darker.

In the kitchen

Preparation and cooking: Simply wash small leaves and steam in just the water remaining on the leaves. For larger leaves, fold in half and pull away the central stem. Young tender leaves make an excellent salad green, while tougher stalks can be braised.

Storage and freezing: Keeps in the fridge for a few days. Do not freeze.

♥ High in iron, calcium and vitamin A.

Calendar

- Cover late-sown crops with cloches when frosts start.
- Sow summer varieties Mar–May.
- Sow winter varieties Aug–Sep.
- Harvest late May–end Oct and Oct–Apr.

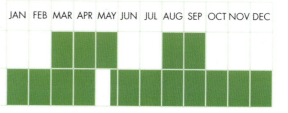

	JAN	FEB	MAR	APR	MAY	JUN	JUL	AUG	SEP	OCT	NOV	DEC
Sowing/ planting time			■	■	■			■	■			
Harvest time	■	■	■	■		■	■	■	■	■	■	■

Squashes

Members of the gourd family, which includes pumpkins, summer squashes mature during the summer and early autumn and are best picked and eaten straight away as they tend to be softer skinned and do not store well. Winter squashes mature mid to late autumn and need a long season to ripen the fruit.

Varieties

SUMMER SQUASH
Patty pan 'Scallop Mixed': An unusual flat yellow or white fruit with a scalloped edge. The small, young fruits can be eaten raw or cooked as you would courgettes.

WINTER SQUASH
Butternut 'Avalon': Wonderfully flavoured with a trailing habit and good long-term storage.
Pumpkin 'Dill's Atlantic Giant': The one to grow if you want a record-breaking monster.
Pumpkin 'Mars F1': Produces good 2.75 kg/ 6lb fruits ideal for carving for Halloween and eating.

Vegetable spaghetti 'Hasta La Pasta F1': A great winter squash that produces oval, orange fruits; inside, the spaghetti-like flesh makes a refreshing, healthy alternative to spaghetti.

Growing tips

Sowing and planting
Squashes are tender plants so should be sown in containers – one seed, on its edge, to a small 9cm/3½in pot or cell in a cell tray, filled with multi-purpose or a John Innes seed or No. 1 compost. Place the pots on a warm windowsill or in a propagator.

Check them daily as they are quick to germinate and, if too warm, the stems will stretch rapidly making them top heavy. Move the seedlings to the greenhouse or a cold frame to grow on, but watch out for slugs as they love young squash plants.

When all danger of frost has passed, the squashes can be planted outside. Space the trailing varieties at least 1.2m/4ft apart and bush varieties about 60cm/2ft apart.

- Place developing squashes on a piece of wood or tile to keep the fruit off the soil and prevent rot setting in.
- Mulch the crop with straw or grass clippings to avoid moisture loss.

Growing on

Squashes require a good fertile soil. They could even be grown on an old muck heap, as long as the manure is well rotted and no longer hot. Alternatively, dig a 30cm/12in deep hole with a similar diameter and back fill with some garden compost or well-rotted manure. Heap a half mix of soil and compost on top and form a mound. Put the plant into a hole made in the top of the heap, deep enough to support the stem. You may need to tie the stem to a short stake, as strong winds may shred the leaves of the young plant or snap the weak stems.

Summer squashes are best harvested when small: the round ones when only tennis ball size and the longer ones at about 10–13cm/4–5in long. They grow very fast so, if you have several plants, you may find yourself picking squash every day. If the fruits are left to grow, the plants tend to stop flowering as much.

Winter squashes, such as pumpkins, may take some time to start flowering. Leave the stems to trail naturally for 3–4.5m/10–15ft, then nip the growing tip off to encourage side shoots to form along the stem. These will produce a lot more flowers, usually male flowers at first but then female ones. At this stage, you should start to see one or two fruits setting. If you are aiming for a really large pumpkin, remove the growing tip about two or three leaves beyond the fruit. Remove the growing tips of other side shoots too, to encourage all the plant's energy into the fruits you want to grow.

In the kitchen

Beneath the hard exterior of a winter squash hides succulent sweet flesh. Summer squashes need to be used quickly and there are numerous recipes for this versatile vegetable.

Preparation and cooking: Cook winter squashes with the skin on, so the skin can be removed easily when it is soft and pliable. Cut into wedges, lay skin-side down on an oiled tray and bake until soft and slightly charred. The skins should come off easily. Chop the flesh into cubes and use in pasta dishes, risotto or lasagne, or purée into a sauce, soup or mash. Roasting brings out the natural sweetness and intensifies the colour.

Summer squashes can be sliced and cooked in butter, added to casseroles, made into soups and roasted in the oven.

Storage and freezing: Winter squashes can be stored for a few months and are best picked as late as possible as you want them to be mature. When there is the risk of colder, damper weather, harvest the fruits and move to a warm room indoors to help set the skin. Keep in the warmth for a couple of days before moving to a cool, dry place to store. Do not freeze.

♥ *High in vitamin A and potassium; useful amounts of vitamin C.*

Feed occasionally with a general purpose fertiliser to encourage good leaf colour and fruit growth.

Winter squashes may not be ready until October after the plant has died back.

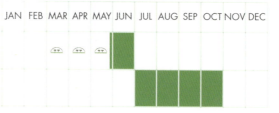

Calendar

- Make early sowings of winter squashes late Mar–Apr under cover.
- Plant outisde end May–June when frosts are over.
- Harvest Jul–Oct.

	JAN	FEB	MAR	APR	MAY	JUN	JUL	AUG	SEP	OCT	NOV	DEC
Sowing/ planting time			🌱	🌱	🌱	■						
Harvest time							■	■	■	■		

SPICY SQUASH

Squashes are a great vegetable to grow and even better to eat, but it can be a challenge to find enough ways to present them to keep the family interested. This tasty recipe is especially good as an addition to the traditional Christmas spread.

1 butternut or other winter squash, halved and deseeded
50g/2oz unsalted butter
4 tsp brown sugar
handful of fresh coriander, chopped, or 1 tsp coriander seeds, crushed
pinch of turmeric
2.5cm/1in piece of ginger root, peeled and finely chopped (optional)
salt and freshly ground black pepper

1 Preheat the oven to 200°C/400°F/gas 6/fan oven 180°C. Place the squash in a baking dish with the butter and sugar in the hollow, together with the coriander, turmeric, ginger and salt and pepper.
2 Pour a cupful of hot water into the baking dish around the squash, cover with foil and bake for 45 minutes. Uncover and cook for a further 10 minutes and serve straight from the shell.

ROASTED PUMPKIN AND CHEESE PARCELS

Serves 6

1.5–1.8 kg/3–4lb pumpkin or other squash, cut into sections and deseeded
1 tsp olive oil, for brushing
225g/8oz soft cheese
250g/9oz semi-soft smoked cheese, grated
1 bunch of spring onions, finely chopped
10 fresh sage leaves, chopped
salt and freshly ground black pepper
500g/1¼lb packet of puff pastry
melted butter, for brushing

1 Preheat the oven to 200°C/400°F/gas 6/fan oven 180°C. Brush the cut sides of the pumpkin or squash with olive oil. Place on a baking tray and roast in the oven for about 40–50 minutes. Allow to cool and scrape the flesh from the skin.
2 Mash the flesh in a bowl with the soft cheese, 175g/6oz of the smoked cheese, chopped spring onions and sage. Season to taste.
3 Cut the puff pastry into 20cm/8in lengths and roll each out to 10cm/4in wide and place on an oiled baking tray. Brush the pastry with melted butter. Place a little pumpkin mix on half of each piece of pastry and top with the remaining smoked cheese. Fold the pastry over the filling to form a square. Seal each one and brush with more melted butter. Bake for 15 minutes.

Container growing

Squashes can be grown in a large container. Ideally, one of 60cm/2ft in diameter. Fill the pot with a mix of multi-purpose compost and some garden compost, if possible. Plant one squash plant per pot and place in a warm, sunny spot. Keep it well watered, especially once the fruits begin to form. The trailing squashes will need to be allowed room on the ground or alternatively tie the stems to a wigwam of canes or up a trellis on a wall. Check the stems every day because they grow rapidly and need to be tied in regularly.

Allow pumpkins and other heavy squashes to trail as the weight of the fruit may be too much for a cane structure to support.

Sweetcorn

There is nothing more delightful on a warm summer's evening than eating barbecued home-grown sweetcorn; the juices and melted butter dribbling down your chin. This crop is simple to grow and a great one to involve children in. It does need quite a bit of space, though, so it's not really suitable for small-scale gardening.

Varieties

'Conquest': A reliable sweetcorn with early crops.
'Extra Tender and Sweet': A quick germinating variety said to be superior in taste and having better vigour than other varieties.
'Indian Summer': A supersweet type that is high in sugars and produces red and purple kernels among the yellow ones.

Growing tips

Sweetcorn is a type of maize and it produces its cobs of yellow kernels on very tall 1.8m/6ft stems – one to three cobs per stem. The top of the plant produces tassels, which are the male flowers, the female parts are the silks sticking out of the immature cobs on the plant below the tassels. The pollen from the male part of the flower has to land on the silks to pollinate the female flowers and swell the cobs. This is done by the breeze, which is why sweetcorn needs to be grown in a block, not in a single line.

Sowing and planting

Sweetcorn is best sown under cover to start it growing quickly before planting out. It is a crop that needs a long, warm season to do well. As it does not like root disturbance, sow the seeds into special long, deep pots that open up, which you can buy. Otherwise make your own pots out of rolled-up newspaper or toilet roll tubes. There is no need to remove the newspaper or toilet roll when you plant them out.

Sow two seeds per pot and place in a greenhouse or on a windowsill. In April no extra heat will be necessary. When the seedlings emerge remove the weakest to leave one per pot. Keep the compost moist and grow on in plenty of light.

Growing on

Prepare the soil where the sweetcorn is going to go, when the danger of frost has passed, by adding some well-rotted farmyard manure or garden compost. When the plants are at least 13cm/5in tall, plant them in a block 45cm/18in apart. Water in well.

As the crop grows keep the soil moist, especially when the cobs are forming; drought

Fact file

- Growing your own sweetcorn is better than buying it because it can be eaten fresh when the cobs are still packed with sugar and have not turned to starch.
- Don't grow two or three different sweetcorn varieties together. This can result in cross-pollination which may affect the taste.

In the kitchen

Sweetcorn kept in its husk remains fresh for longer, protects the juicy kernels from bruising and prevents the cob drying out. Inside, the kernels should be tight and plump.

Preparation and cooking: To prepare sweetcorn, remove the outer husks and silky fibres. But you can bake the whole cob including husks in an oven or on the barbecue, which will make the husks even easier to remove. If you want to use only the loose kernels, stand the cob upright on its base and run a sharp knife down the core, slicing them off.

Cook husk-free cobs in deep boiling water for 15 minutes or wrap individually in foil and bake or barbecue until tender. Resist adding salt during cooking as this toughens the kernels. Serve with generous amounts of melting butter. Great fun to chew off the cob, so serve whole or chop into chunks after cooking when the core is soft.

Storage and freezing: Sweetcorn will keep for a couple of days in the fridge but is best eaten as soon as harvested. To freeze, blanch the sweetcorn for 5 minutes, either on the cobs or as loose kernels, then drain and cool. Wrap cobs individually in clingfilm before freezing.
♥ *Good source of fibre and vitamin B.*

BARBECUED SWEETCORN WITH CHILLI AND LIME BUTTER

Serves 4
225g/8oz butter
1 lime
1 fresh red chilli, deseeded and finely chopped
4 corn on the cobs, husks and silks removed

1 Soften the butter in a small bowl. Zest half the lime and squeeze the juice from the whole lime and add to the butter with the chilli. Mix well.
2 Generously smear the cobs with the butter mixture and barbecue or grill until the juices are clear and the cobs are toasted. Baste with any remaining mixture if necessary.
Serve with: Lime wedges to squeeze over.

---

at this stage will cause shrivelled or undeveloped cobs. Pick them when the silks turn dark brown. Peel open a cob and push a fingernail into a kernel. If the juice is creamy the cob is ripe.

Container growing

Sweetcorn is not really suitable for growing in pots because of the need to grow in blocks to ensure pollination. However, three or four large tubs containing three or four plants of sweetcorn could be placed in a group and you may get a few cobs. As sweetcorn is a large leafy plant, it would look stunning in a group of pots on a sunny patio. The sweetcorn could be used to shade an area of the patio or even obscure an eyesore or view of the neighbours. Large pots at least 60cm/2ft diameter will be needed to provide stability against the wind. Fill with a multi-purpose compost or John Innes No. 3, mixed with well-rotted garden compost, if possible, to help retain moisture.

Calendar

- Start in a greenhouse.
- Sow under cover in Apr/May.
- Plant out end May–early Jun, when no frost.
- Tap stems to release pollen Jul.
| Harvest Aug–Sep.

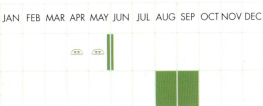

	JAN	FEB	MAR	APR	MAY	JUN	JUL	AUG	SEP	OCT	NOV	DEC
Sowing/ planting time				😴	😴	▌ ▌						
Harvest time								██	██			

Swiss chard

S wiss chard is worth growing just for its decorative leaves and stems and it is delicious to eat, stems and all, being very similar to spinach. A clump can look wonderful in the flower border. Swiss chard is a crop for autumn, winter and spring harvests, at a time when there is little else around. It grows into a clump about 45cm/1½ft high and wide.

Varieties

'Bright Lights': A fabulous mixture of different-coloured chards with stems of white, red, yellow and orange. Delicious to eat and lovely to look at.

Fact file

- The darker the stems the more bitter the taste. The white ones do seem to be the sweetest.
- Germination can take up to 2 weeks.
- A similar crop called rhubarb chard, or ruby chard, has thinner stems than Swiss chard.

Growing tips

Sowing and planting
Swiss chard is not too fussy about soil but it prefers a sunny spot. Sow chard directly where you intend to grow it in a seed drill about 2.5cm/1in deep. Once the seedlings are through thin them out to about 10cm/4in apart and eventually, when they are bigger, to 30cm/12in apart.

Container growing

Swiss chard is best grown in the ground where it has room, but three plants of different coloured 'Bright Lights' in a large pot would be attractive on the patio in summer.

In the kitchen
Swiss chard is a luscious, easy-to-grow green with juicy leaves and vibrant stalks. The colourful stalks and leaf veins are magnificent, but colours can bleed during cooking, tinting your dish.
Preparation and cooking: Cut away the leaves from the fleshy stalks. Cook separately and in different ways. Chard leaves have a slightly bitter earthiness and coarse texture. Use raw or cook as you would spinach, but remember it's more robust in flavour. The crunchy stems can be chopped and sautéed in butter and garlic or braised in wine as a sumptuous side dish.
Storage and freezing: Swiss chard will keep for a few days in the fridge. Do not freeze.
♥ High in vitamins A and C but also contains other vitamins and minerals in smaller amounts.

Calendar

- Harvest 10–12 weeks after sowing.
- Cover early sowings with cloches, or sow into cell trays or pots and plant out once established.

	JAN	FEB	MAR	APR	MAY	JUN	JUL	AUG	SEP	OCT	NOV	DEC
Sowing/ planting time			🌱	■	■	■						
Harvest time	■	■	■					■	■	■	■	■

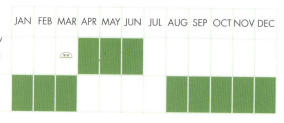

Tomatoes

Strictly speaking a fruit, this popular greenhouse crop can also be grown outside on the patio or plot or even in a hanging basket. There are hundreds of varieties ranging from the tiny cherry tomatoes to the huge beefsteak types. They are great value because gardeners can grow varieties that are not bred for shelf life but are so much tastier.

Varieties

Out of so many varieties producing delicious fruit in various shapes, sizes and colours, here are a few worth a mention.

'Costoluto Fiorentino': A fantastic beefsteak tomato with fruits up to 10cm/4in in diameter. Renowned for its wonderful flesh and great flavour. Ideal for tarts and tomato sauces. Best grown in a greenhouse.

'Ferline': A must for gardeners who have problems with tomato blight, as it has good resistance to this fungal disease.

'Sungold': A really popular cherry tomato that can be grown in a greenhouse or outside. It produces masses of tiny, very sweet orange-red fruits. The skins are very thin too which does mean they split easily, but the taste makes up for it.

'Tumbler': A perfect tomato to grow in a hanging basket. It produces tiny cherry-red tomatoes and can be put in a basket with some bedding plants for an attractive and tasty display.

Fact file

- Seed germination can take up to 10 days.
- Don't let tomatoes dry out at the roots as it can cause blossom-end rot on the fruits. The base of the tomatoes turns black and is sunken.
- When a plant has reached the top of the greenhouse or has about seven trusses of fruit, remove the growing tip.
- Growing marigolds with tomatoes is said to keep whitefly at bay.

Growing tips

Sowing and planting

Fill small pots or trays with multi-purpose compost and sprinkle seeds over the surface. Cover with 6mm/¼in of compost and water lightly. Place in a propagator or on a warm windowsill at a temperature of about 70°F/21°C.

Once the seedlings are through remove from the propagator and put on a light warm windowsill or in a heated greenhouse. When large enough to handle, move the seedlings into individual 9cm/3½in pots. Grow on in a warm well-lit spot. When they start to show signs of flower buds, plant them into their final pots or growbags inside a greenhouse or polytunnel if there is still a danger of frost. At the end of May or beginning of June they can go outside in a sheltered, sunny spot.

In the kitchen

Fresh from the vine, tomatoes have a heady aroma and an irresistible combination of sweetness, acidity and refreshing juiciness. They come in a medley of shades, sizes and sweetness. Small, sweeter and firmer cherry tomatoes hold their own in salads, while larger, more watery varieties can be used for cooking.

Preparation and cooking: A tomato salad can make a grand centrepiece for an outdoor lunch or picnic. Partner ripe tomatoes with fresh basil leaves, mozzarella cheese, olive oil and plenty of seasoning. Make it more interesting by combining different varieties, contrasting shape, colour, texture and flavour.

Tomatoes are usually best skinned before cooking. Make a cross cut at the base of each tomato and plunge them into boiling water for a couple of minutes. The skins will start to loosen and peel off.

Soups, purées, ketchups and sauces freeze well and can be enjoyed into winter, when the abundance of tomatoes seems a distant memory. If you find you have a glut, think ahead. A large batch of chutney will see the year out and make excellent gifts.

Storage and freezing: Store for a few days in the fridge. Do not freeze unless cooked.

♥ Rich source of lycopene.

HERBY CHEESE TOMATOES

Serves 1–2

2–4 medium-sized tomatoes
100g/4oz white crumbly cheese, such as Lancashire, Feta or Wensleydale
a couple of leaves of basil and mint, finely chopped
large sprig of parsley, finely chopped
few drops of fresh lemon juice
sea salt and freshly ground black pepper
olive oil, to garnish

1 With a sharp knife, cut a slice off the top of each tomato. Scoop out the seeds with a teaspoon. Place upside down on a plate to drain.
2 Crumble up the cheese and mix with the herbs and lemon juice and seasoning, and stuff into the tomatoes.
3 Drizzle the olive oil over the tomatoes.

Growing on

Tomatoes are either cordon types, which require the support of canes, or bush, which do not need any support. Mist the flowers during the day to improve pollination and fruit set of the flowers. As cordon tomatoes grow tie them in with string and remove any side shoots that form in the leaf joints. Keep the plants well watered and when the first fruits start to set, feed with a liquid tomato fertiliser weekly.

In the height of summer keep the greenhouse well ventilated on hot sunny days and if necessary provide some shade.

Calendar

- Sow greenhouse tomatoes very early Feb.
- Sow outdoor tomatoes under cover Mar–Apr. Plant out end May–Jun.
- Harvest Jul–Oct.

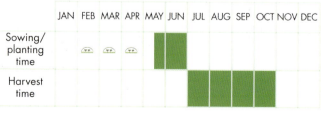

	JAN	FEB	MAR	APR	MAY	JUN	JUL	AUG	SEP	OCT	NOV	DEC
Sowing/ planting time		☙	☙	☙	■	■						
Harvest time							■	■	■	■		

CHEESY TOMATO TARTLETS

This recipe can make 20 individual tartlets as a starter or snack, or larger ones. If you don't fancy making the pastry, use a ready-made shortcrust instead.

For the pastry:
225g/8oz plain flour
1/2 tsp salt
50g/2oz lard
50g/2oz butter
100g/4oz Cheddar cheese, grated
2 tbsp water, chilled
beaten egg, for brushing
For the filling:
2 eggs, beaten
1 tbsp double cream
100g/4oz tomato purée
3 tsp chopped chives
For the topping:
50g/2oz Parmesan cheese, grated
salt and freshly ground black pepper
50g/2oz wholewheat breadcrumbs
450g/1lb tomatoes, skinned and sliced

1 Grease two 25cm/10in tart tins or individual tartlet baking tins.
2 To make the pastry, sieve the flour and salt together into a bowl. Cut the lard and butter into cubes and rub lightly into the flour, lifting the mixture to add air, until it resembles breadcrumbs, or use a food processor. Add the grated Cheddar cheese.
3 Make a well in the middle of the mixture and stir in enough water to produce a soft pastry. Cover the bowl with clingfilm and place in the fridge for about 30 minutes to rest.
4 Meanwhile, make the filling, by mixing all the ingredients together.
5 To make the topping, combine the breadcrumbs and the Parmesan.
6 Preheat the oven to 200°C/400°F/gas 6/fan oven 180°C. Roll out the pastry and line the tartlet baking tin. Prick over the base of the pastry. Brush with egg and bake blind for about 10 minutes, being careful not to allow the edges to brown too much.
7 Reduce the oven temperature to 180°C/350°F/gas 4/fan oven 160°C. Spoon the filling into the tarts, leaving room for expansion. Arrange the tomatoes on top and sprinkle on the topping. Bake for a further 10 minutes or so checking regularly. Remove the tarts once the filling is firm in the centre. Serve warm.

Container growing

Tomatoes are best grown in containers in a proprietary compost as they tend to be more susceptible to blight. Growbags are ideal and have room for three tomatoes per bag. They can also be grown in individual 38cm/15in pots, filled with compost from a growbag, or the small bush tomatoes will do well in a well-watered hanging basket. Plant up a 30cm/12in basket with one small bush tomato, such as 'Tumbler', with some marigolds and perhaps a plant of basil and you will have a very useful, attractive basket.

Turnips

Varieties

'Aramis': A purple top turnip ideal for growing close together to produce small roots.
'Tokyo Cross': A white turnip with an RHS Award of Garden Merit. Can harvest 35 days from sowing.

Growing tips

Sowing and planting

Turnips can be sown in February if protected with cloches or a polytunnel. The main sowing period of March to April will produce a crop as early as May.

They like a good soil that is slightly alkaline, so a dressing of lime will be necessary if you have acidic soil. Sprinkle some fertiliser, such as Growmore, or chicken manure on the plot a week before sowing.

Sow the seed thinly into drills 1cm/½in deep that have first been watered. The rows should be about 23cm/9in apart, but autumn-sown turnips can be 8cm/3in apart as you want plenty of leaves. If sowing in spring or summer, thin to 13cm/5in apart.

Growing on

Water well, as dry soil causes woody 'roots'. As soon as the turnips are large, start lifting them.

Home-grown turnips are the best to eat. They can be harvested when they reach golf ball size and eaten raw in salads, rather like radishes, or cooked in many ways. They are also fast to mature and have a long sowing season. Their leaves can be harvested in spring as a delicious alternative to spinach.

Fact file

• Turnips are members of the brassica family, which includes the cabbage and cauliflower. The part that is eaten is not the root but the swollen base of the stem.
• Watch out for flea beetle, which attacks the seedlings, peppering them with holes. Apply insecticide spray or powder, or cover with horticultural fleece.

In the kitchen

Preparation and cooking: Scrub turnips and trim well, removing the skin only if tough. Early harvested sprouting leaves and stalks can be used like broccoli. Use young when their sweetness is at its peak. Later in the season, their stronger earthy flavour bolsters stews and soups.
Storage: Stores well and will see you through the winter if kept somewhere cool, dark and dry.
♥ A good source of vitamins; also contains high levels of phosphorus, a mineral that is a component of DNA.

Calendar

• Harvest autumn-sown turnip tops Mar–Apr.
• Sow Feb under cover.
• Sow Mar–Sep outside.
• Harvest May–Oct.

	JAN	FEB	MAR	APR	MAY	JUN	JUL	AUG	SEP	OCT	NOV	DEC
Sowing/ planting time		✿	■	■	■	■	■	■	■			
Harvest time			■	■	■	■	■	■	■	■		

how to grow your own
Herbs

Basil

The popularity of Mediterranean cooking has put basil at the top of the list of home-grown herbs. There are so many great varieties to grow, many with wonderful scents and subtle differences in flavour, not to mention leaf shapes and colours. Quite a tender herb, as it comes from sunnier climes, basil is nonetheless quite easy to grow.

Varieties

'Nufar F1': Generally more productive than 'Genovese'.
'Purple Ruffles' and 'Red Rubin': Both varieties have attractive red leaves.
Sweet basil ('Genovese'): Freely available from most catalogues and is the classic culinary type.
'Sweet Thai': Pretty pink flowers and small leaves.

Growing tips

Given gentle warmth in a propagator heated to 21°C/71°F, basil germinates easily. However, they are prone to damping off disease, which causes the seedlings to collapse. Sowing in cell trays can limit losses by restricting the spread of the disease.

Sow a small pinch of seeds into each cell filled with multi-purpose compost and cover with a fine layer of compost. Water well with a mist spray and place in a propagator. Remove the lid as soon as the seedlings emerge, and water as required. Once most of them have germinated, take the cell tray out of the propagator and place on a warm, light windowsill or in a greenhouse heated to around 15°C/60°F to grow on.

If seedlings become leggy, pinch out the growing tips to encourage branching. Basil can be propagated using cuttings, so the tips need not be wasted – dib them into pots filled with gritty compost.

When large enough to handle, plant a cell of seedlings as one plant into a 9cm/3½ in pot, moving into a 13cm/5in pot before the plants become pot bound. Alternatively, plant outside in a warm, sheltered place, once all danger of frost has passed.

Container growing

Basil grows very well in pots in a sunny, sheltered spot. It is also very convenient to have a pot close to the kitchen so you can harvest fresh leaves whenever you need them.

Grow your plants either in 13cm/5in pots, as above, or in larger containers alongside other herbs such as marjoram and parsley. Add some gritty sand to the compost to ensure good drainage and feed regularly with a liquid fertiliser to maintain growth. As basil likes to be warm, grow a pot or two on your kitchen windowsill. Keep pinching the tips out to use in cooking and the plant will become bushier and produce more tender stems to harvest.

In the kitchen

Lush green leaves, bursting with a pungent aniseed flavour and fragrance, make basil the cook's favourite herb.

Basil has an affinity with Mediterranean dishes and vegetables such as tomatoes, peppers and courgettes. The sweetness also sparks up dressing and marinades – sprinkle torn up leaves on sliced tomatoes and mozzarella cheese and drizzle with olive oil for a quick, tasty salad.

♥ *Contains useful amounts of vitamin A, vitamin C, iron and calcium.*

Calendar

- Sow seeds Mar–Apr.
- Plant out end May–Jun when no danger of frost.
- Take cuttings Jun–Jul from pinched out tips.
- Harvest Jun–Oct.

	JAN	FEB	MAR	APR	MAY	JUN	JUL	AUG	SEP	OCT	NOV	DEC
Sowing/ planting time			🌱	🌱		■						
Harvest time						■	■	■	■	■		

Sweet bay (*Laurus nobilis*) is a handsome small tree with glossy green leaves. It can be clipped into many shapes, grown as a standard plant with a clear stem or as a bushy shrub. It has been used for thousands of years for medicinal and ritual purposes and was used by the ancient Greeks to signify brilliance and wisdom, hence the laurel wreath.

Varieties

Bay trees can be grown as standards. These are cultivated as single-stem trees with the lower branches removed gradually until a desired length or leg of stem has been achieved. The top of the plant is then allowed to produce a bushy head.

Growing tips

Bay is difficult to grow from seed, although you can sow it in pots or seed trays and keep moist but not wet at 21°C/65°F. Germination can take ten days or six months! Cuttings taken in early summer need high humidity so use a heated propagator; even so they are not easy and the inexperienced will do better to buy a plant.

Bay needs plenty of water to thrive and, although pretty hardy, the standard trees can be damaged by very hard frosts, snow or biting winds. Choose a sunny spot, although semi-shade is tolerated, but make sure that the plant will be sheltered from cold winds.

Improve the soil with plenty of organic matter prior to planting in the ground and provide standard plants with a stake until well established to avoid wind rock.

Apply a top dressing of fertiliser, such as Growmore, or pelleted chicken manure, around the roots each spring and then top this with a water-retaining mulch or well rotted compost.

Look out for scale insects, which look like little brown limpets, on the stems and underside of the leaves. Spraying with an insecticide may be necessary if attacks are severe. Bay sucker is another pest, which causes the edges of the leaves to thicken, turn yellow and curl. The pests hide in the folds and feed on the sap. Pick off and destroy affected leaves.

Container growing

Bay will grow perfectly well in pots providing it is well fed and watered. Plant in a large container using a gritty compost, preferably John Innes No. 3, and water regularly during dry spells. Feed every seven to ten days in the summer with a liquid feed and, at the start of the season, replace a few centimetres of compost from the top of the pot with fresh material. As an alternative to liquid feeding, add some controlled-release fertiliser pellets to the compost to maintain healthy growth.

In the kitchen

Bay leaves form the backbone of the bouquet garni and numerous liquid-rich, slow-cooked dishes. The leaves are too tough to eat and are used whole to impart their flavour and bring herbal depth to stocks, stews and slow-cooked sauces. Bay also infuses a lovely woody warmth to milk or cream for use in custard and desserts.

Freshly picked leaves release more aromatic oils resulting in a deeper flavour, but are also excellent dried as a store cupboard essential.

♥ *A tea made with bay leaves is said to help improve digestion and promote a good appetite.*

Calendar

- Protect with fleece in winter.
- Clip spring and Jul to maintain shape.
- Plant container-grown trees at any time of year.
- Harvest all year.

	JAN	FEB	MAR	APR	MAY	JUN	JUL	AUG	SEP	OCT	NOV	DEC
Sowing/ planting time												
Harvest time												

Chives

One of the prettiest members of the onion family, chives are a treat in the ornamental garden as well as in the vegetable plot or herb garden. Unfussy and easy to grow, they can be harvested for much of the year and in late spring or early summer produce beautiful fluffy heads of pink, purple or white flowers.

Varieties

The common chive (Allium schoenoprasum) has thin leaves and pink flowers and a mild taste and scent of onion. Garlic, or Chinese, chives (A. tuberosum) have broader leaves and white flowers, and a distinctive, though mild, garlic taste and scent. Garlic chives look more robust than their cousin and grow taller to around 40cm/16in, but both are very hardy.

Growing tips

Sow seeds indoors in spring in a propagator heated to 18°C/65°F, sowing a pinch of seeds to each cell in a tray, and grow the resulting clump on as one plant. Chives will grow in most soils and situations, but prefer a spot in semi-shade or full sun for part, but not all, of the day. They like a moist soil, so dig in plenty of well-rotted garden compost, old potting compost or manure prior to planting.

Every two or three years in the spring, dig up established clumps and divide them keeping the best sections and discarding the rest, or using spare sections to increase stocks. Replant straight away.

Water well between April and September when the weather is dry, or the quality of the leaves will suffer.

Since chives are herbaceous perennials, they will die down with the first frosts. However, the harvesting season can be extended by lifting a clump in the autumn and potting up into a pot just large enough to take the root ball. Place the chives in a light, frost-free position, such as in a greenhouse, polytunnel or windowsill, and you should be able to harvest leaves for an extra month or so.

Container growing

Chives can be grown in pots, windowboxes and hanging baskets provided that they receive enough water while growing. As they make a neat clump and are not invasive, they can be grown with other herbs.

The choice of compost is not too critical, but if using a peat or coir-based compost, add some water-holding gel to help prevent the plants from drying out. John Innes No. 3 is a good compost as it retains water well and is heavy, so gives stability to the container.

In the kitchen

Use the slender leaves in a variety of dishes for a subtle hint of onion or garlic. The flowerless stems are more flavoursome but the flowers are edible too, and make a pretty garnish for salads. Chives provide a lively savoury taste that can be used to replace salt and are particularly good with fish, eggs and dairy. Use raw or lightly cooked in sauces. Snip with scissors or chop finely and sprinkle on soups or salads just before serving.

♥ *Chives have antiseptic properties and are said to improve appetite and digestion.*

Calendar

- Sow Apr–May in warm conditions under cover.
- Divide clumps Mar–Apr every 2–3 years.
- Water well Apr–Sep.
- Harvest Apr–Oct.

	JAN	FEB	MAR	APR	MAY	JUN	JUL	AUG	SEP	OCT	NOV	DEC
Sowing/ planting time				🌱	🌱							
Harvest time				■	■	■	■	■	■	■		

Coriander has a unique flavour that you either love or hate, but since it has been in use for at least 3,000 years, it seems that most people must love it! The attractive round, golden seeds and parsley-like leaves are common ingredients in both Mexican and Indian dishes. It is not a difficult plant to grow in your herb garden.

Varieties

Most seed catalogues offer the standard coriander, *Coriandrum sativum*, although you may occasionally see lemon coriander and an unusual sweeter variety called 'Confetti'.

Growing tips

This tender annual herb prefers a very well-drained soil so avoid heavy clays or other cold, wet soils. If your garden does tend to sit wet for long periods, grow your coriander in pots instead.

Sow the large seeds where they are to grow in May, so that the frosts are over by the time the seedlings are through, and protect them with a cloche for the first few weeks. Sow later in colder areas.

Alternatively, sow one seed into each cell of a cell tray and transplant into the soil or pots once the plants are well established, but before they become pot bound. For the best possible start, either keep the trays in a propagator heated to 15°C/60°F or place on a warm windowsill. Coriander can bolt if under stress so take care to keep the plants well watered and avoid damaging roots when transplanting.

Plants grow to 60–90cm/2–3ft including the attractive wispy white flower head. When the seed heads are nearly ripe, they can be cut and popped into a paper bag to dry fully.

Coriander is short-lived and once it has flowered and set seeds will die. So sow regularly – every three to four weeks – if you want fresh supplies throughout the summer.

Container growing

Delicate-looking coriander is ideal for pots providing that the compost is not allowed to dry out too much. Check regularly during the summer and top up as required – you may well find that watering every day is necessary. The seeds could be sown directly into the container in which they are to grow, but will be easier to take care of in the early stages if sown into cell trays and planted once well established.

Feed three weeks after potting with a liquid fertiliser and at ten to 14 day intervals until the seeds start to ripen. Some staking may be required, especially once the flower heads have formed.

In the kitchen

A distinctive soft herb with a powerful aroma and taste, coriander is associated with Middle Eastern and Oriental cuisine where it is used in much the same way as parsley.

A simple salsa of diced tomatoes, red onion and a handful of fresh, chopped coriander makes a refreshing condiment. The leaves discolour, wilt and lose flavour fast, so add at the last minute.

♥ *Good for the digestion and improves appetite.*

Calendar

- Sow outside May–Jul.
- Protect under cloches in May when still a danger of frost.
- Sow in pots in spring in the warmth.
- Harvest leaves Jun–Oct.

	JAN	FEB	MAR	APR	MAY	JUN	JUL	AUG	SEP	OCT	NOV	DEC
Sowing/ planting time				🌱	🌱	■	■					
Harvest time						■	■	■	■	■		

Dill

In the kitchen

Dill has a subtle fragrance of fennel, and the prettiness, without the punch. The fragile fronds get lost during cooking so it is best used raw. Tear up and add to marinades and dressings, or use as a pretty, feathered garnish. The delicate herb bruises easily and discolours once cut. Treat gently, and only chop with firm strokes or a sharp knife. It has an affinity with fish and creamy soft cheeses. Generously stuff into the cavity before baking or poaching whole fish or mix into soft cheese and pile on toast. Add seeds to coleslaw. It is possible to freeze the leaves but they should be used within three months.

♥ *Dill seeds are very good for the digestion.*

Similar in appearance to fennel, dill is an attractive plant with feathery foliage. It can be grown in the flower border for decoration and also to attract beneficial insects that love the yellow flower heads. Dill belongs to the parsley family, Umbellifera, one of the largest plant families that also includes fennel, angelica, carrots and parsnips.

Varieties

There is only one type of dill (*Anethum graveolens*), which is thought to originate from the Mediterranean and western Asia, although its true origins are unclear. The name dill is said to derive from the Anglo-Saxon name dylie and refers to the soothing effect it can have on the digestion. The species name graveolens means 'strong smelling' and is shared by other plants with pungent leaves such as rue (*Ruta graveolens*).

Growing tips

Like many herbs from warmer climes, dill prefers a sunny spot and well-drained soil, in fact it is grown in much the same way as fennel (see page 85). Sow where the dill is to grow, avoiding soil which is very rich in nutrients (recently manured). Choose a spot sheltered from strong winds. If you are allowing your fennel to set seed, try to grow the two herbs far apart from each other to avoid cross pollination or the flavour of both may be affected.

Thin seedlings to leave 23–30cm/9–12in between plants and water well during dry spells. Leaves can be harvested as soon as the plants are big enough. They quickly lose their pungency, so should be used immediately. Harvest the seeds when the seed head turns brown. Break open the heads to release the seeds and dry and store in an airtight container.

Container growing

It is possible to grow this attractive plant in a container. Grow in a John Innes No. 1 or 2 compost and water well during dry spells. Dill makes a good centrepiece to a pot, with other smaller herbs or colourful bedding plants around it, and placed in a sheltered spot.

Calendar

- To maintain supplies sow a batch every 3–4 weeks May–Jul.
- Harvest dill leaves late Jun–Oct.
- Harvest seeds Aug–Oct.

	JAN	FEB	MAR	APR	MAY	JUN	JUL	AUG	SEP	OCT	NOV	DEC
Sowing/ planting time					■	■	■					
Harvest time						■	■	■	■	■	■	

Fennel

If you love the taste of aniseed, you'll love fennel, however this pretty plant with its feathery foliage and heads of yellow flowers is well worth growing for its decorative effect alone. The whole plant, including the swollen leaf bases, which have increased in popularity, is edible. Even the seeds have both medicinal and culinary uses.

Varieties

There are two main types: Florence fennel, with green leaves, and bronze fennel with beautiful deep-coloured foliage. There are many varieties of Florence fennel that have been bred for their superior taste, yield or resistance to bolting. Try 'Mantevano' or 'Montebianco', both with large, white crunchy bulbs, or 'Victoria' or 'Amigo F1', both resistant to bolting.

Growing tips

Fennel is not the easiest plant to grow as a vegetable, as if it becomes too dry it can bolt very easily before developing the swollen bulb.

The essential requirement is a well-drained, but moisture retentive soil. If plants suffer root disturbance, are too cold or dry out they are likely to bolt and the leaf bases will fail to form.

Dig in plenty of organic matter in autumn prior to sowing and sow from April to June where the plants are to grow. Water regularly and remove weeds as they appear, to prevent competition. As plants develop mulch with additional organic matter, such as well-rotted garden compost or manure, to retain water in the soil during the summer.

For earlier crops it is possible to sow into cell trays in a warm greenhouse in February to March and to transplant into the plot once well established. Harden the seedlings off first to get them used to cooler temperatures and once transplanted, cover with cloches. Similarly you can sow in the autumn and overwinter plants in the greenhouse.

The young plants can be planted out in the border of a greenhouse or polytunnel to grow on. In either case always move the plants on while the seedlings are still small and before they become pot bound.

Earthing up established plants can help to improve the whiteness of the stems.

Container growing

Fennel is not suited to growing in a container unless it is a very large pot.

In the kitchen

The feathery tops of the fennel plant can be used as a soft herb to add sweetness and exotic aniseed aromas to dishes. Its dominant aniseed flavour and slight citrus note complements fish perfectly. However, use this herb sparingly as it can be overpowering and mask subtle flavours. Once cut, the fronds discolour and become bitter, so simply tear into dishes when required, minimising cutting and bruising. Fragile feathered leaves cannot withstand much heat so add towards the end of cooking or use raw in salads and dressings.

The fennel bulb can be trimmed and grated into salads, brushed with oil and roasted in a hot oven for about 20 minutes, or sliced into casseroles.

♥ Good for constipation, colic and digestion.

Calendar

- Prepare soil in the autumn for planting out seedlings in spring.
- Sow Feb–Mar under cover or Apr–Jun where the plants are to grow.
- Harvest late Jun–Nov.

		JAN	FEB	MAR	APR	MAY	JUN	JUL	AUG	SEP	OCT	NOV	DEC
Sowing/ planting time			🌱	🌱	■	■	■				🌱	🌱	
Harvest time								■	■	■	■	■	

Marjoram

O. vulgare is found growing wild in parts of the British Isles. The delicate leaves come in shades of green and gold, depending on the variety, with small decorative clusters of flowers in shades of purple, pink and white. Good varieties to try include the golden marjoram 'Aureum' and 'Greek' oregano, which has felty grey-green leaves.

Growing tips

Common oregano can be grown from seed sown in the spring. Sow a pinch of the tiny seeds into each cell of a cell tray, filled with well-watered multi-purpose compost. Don't cover the seeds with any more compost but mist over with water before placing in a propagator heated to 15°C/60°F. Check daily to ensure that the tiny seedlings do not dry out and uncover once the majority have come through. Germination can take a few weeks so be patient and keep watering.

Grow the cluster of seedlings on as one plant and when they are well established, transplant them as one outdoors. The yellow-leaved variety, 'Aureum', is best grown in semi-shade to prevent the leaves from becoming 'bleached' in the sunshine. Otherwise, choose a well-drained site in full sun; moisture retentive soil is essential. Mulching plants with a layer of fine grit can help to keep winter wet from around the crown of the plant.

Most types of marjoram can be propagated by taking softwood cuttings in the spring. Alternatively, root cuttings can be taken in late summer; the clumps can also be divided up and replanted in the spring or the autumn.

Container growing

Seedlings of marjoram or oregano can be transplanted as a clump into large pots and left in a sunny spot on the patio; keep well watered.

Marjoram and oregano are simply different species of the same plant – *Origanum* – but confusion abounds around which is which, since the same plants have many different names. However, these pretty, easy-to-grow plants are well worth growing as an edging in the flower border or in a container.

Varieties

Oregano (*Origanum vulgare*) and pot marjoram (*O. onites*) are essential herbs for the kitchen. Although they originate mainly from the Mediterranean, many are reasonably hardy and

In the kitchen

Light green marjoram is sweet and delicate whereas oregano is more pungent. Both can be used in the same way but be more sparing with oregano. They are delicious sprinkled over pizza or pasta dishes, or crushed with garlic, lemon juice and olive oil as a Mediterranean marinade for chicken or fish. It is one of the few herbs that can withstand drying without losing its flavour.
♥ *An infusion of marjoram helps relieve a cold.*

Calendar

- To maintain supplies, sow a batch every 3–4 weeks May–Jul.
- Take softwood cuttings in spring; root cuttings late summer.
- Harvest leaves late Jun–Oct.

	JAN	FEB	MAR	APR	MAY	JUN	JUL	AUG	SEP	OCT	NOV	DEC
Sowing/ planting time					🌱	🌱	🌱					
Harvest time							■	■	■	■		

Mint

Mints are fascinating plants – there are so many varieties with very different scents, flavours, leaf shapes and shades. As with sages there are some wonderful fruity selections such as apple, pineapple and lemon mints as well as the more familiar spearmint and the deliciously scented chocolate and ginger mints.

Varieties

There are many varieties of mint. Common mint (*Mentha vulgaris*) is the most popular, but you could also try apple mint (*M. suaveolans*) or spearmint (*M. spicata*). Pennyroyal (*M. pulegium*) is very different in appearance. It is a pretty little ground-hugging type producing tiny mauve flowers in summer and is ideal for growing in rock gardens or between cracks and crevices in paths and patios. It has a strong scent of peppermint and should be used sparingly in cooking.

In the kitchen

Different mints complement different dishes: ginger mint is delicious in tomato recipes; lemon mint gives fruit dishes a lift, and a sprig of mint in the water is a must when cooking new potatoes.

To make a small pot of mint sauce, chop several young tips of spearmint, mix with vinegar to cover, and just under ¼ tsp sugar.

Mint leaves store well either by drying or freezing, providing a supply throughout the winter. Freeze the best shoots in small bunches in freezer bags, or freeze shoot tips in ice cubes to drop into the cooking pan as required.

♥ *Mint leaves infused in boiling water are good for the digestive system and can relieve indigestion.*

Growing tips

Most mints spread using runners, modified roots that run along just below the surface, rooting and shooting as they go. This means that they can be highly invasive, especially if grown among other perennial plants. It is often recommended that they be grown in a bucket or large pot buried in the ground, rim proud of the soil, to restrict the roots. Even so, care is needed not to allow the plants to escape.

Mints are herbaceous perennials, meaning that they die down once the frosts start in the winter and shoot again in the spring. The foliage tends to deteriorate after flowering so removing the blooms will prolong harvesting.

Container growing

Mints are well suited to growing in pots in a gritty compost such as John Innes No. 3. Add a controlled-release fertiliser when planting to help maintain growth. If the plant starts to 'run out of steam' then give a liquid feed during the growing season. Place containers in a semi-shaded spot or a sunny spot if the plant has coloured leaves.

The roots will quickly fill the container and so every couple of years lift and split the plants. Remove the plant from the pot and force a spade through the roots, chopping off sections that can be replanted in fresh compost.

Calendar

- Lift sections of root in autumn and pot up. Place in greenhouse or on windowsill to provide green shoots for the kitchen.
- Plant Mar–Sep.
- Harvest May–Oct.

	JAN	FEB	MAR	APR	MAY	JUN	JUL	AUG	SEP	OCT	NOV	DEC
Sowing/ planting time			■	■	■	■	■	■	■			
Harvest time					■	■	■	■	■	■		

Parsley

Of all our herbs, parsley is perhaps the one grown most profusely on the allotment, being useful as a garnish and an ingredient in so many traditional dishes. Rich in iron and vitamin C, parsley is also a valuable source of minerals and has been used in traditional medicine to aid digestion and cure urinary infections.

Varieties

Parsley (*Petroselinum crispum*) falls into two main categories, the common, curled-leaf parsley, most popular in the UK, and the flat-leaved type, also known as French or broad-leaf parsley, commonly used in Europe and the Middle East. Both types are easy to grow from seed. Less well known, yet offered by many major seed companies, is Hamburg parsley, a deep-rooted plant that looks much like a parsnip, tastes like parsley and the root is always used cooked. Although perennial, this plant is generally grown as an annual, however, the other parsleys, which are grown for their leaves, are biennial.

Growing tips

As French and curled-leaf parsleys are biennial, it is necessary to grow a fresh supply every year. Germination can be slow and erratic, but in the case of the leafy types is improved if seeds are sown early in the year in cell trays of multi-purpose compost and placed in a propagator heated to 18°C/65°F. Thin out, then, plant out once well established without disturbing the roots.

If sowing directly into the soil – necessary with Hamburg parsley, which does not like to be transplanted – use a cloche or a black polythene mulch to warm the soil first and cover with the cloche again after sowing.

Sow a batch once a month from February to June to provide a succession of cropping.

Maintain watering during the growing season to prevent wilting during dry spells and look out for carrot fly if you have carrot plants, to which parsley is related, close by. Growing in semi-shade reduces the likelihood of bolting and is also said to help deter the carrot fly.

Harvest the leaves as required and, when they are at their best, freeze some in food bags or chop and freeze as ice cubes. Dig up the roots of Hamburg parsley in the autumn and store in boxes of slightly damp sand.

Container growing

Both French and curled-leaf parsleys are perfect for growing in clumps in pots on a windowsill or as part of a larger pot of herbs on the patio, as long as they are kept well watered.

In the kitchen

Its fresh, grassy taste enhances most savoury dishes as an ingredient or garnish. Curled leaf is more common in British cooking but the flat leaved is now widely available. Like most soft herbs parsley discolours when used, so finely chop as needed and add just before serving.

Chopped parsley, crushed garlic and melted butter are a match made in heaven. Combine over a gentle heat for a simple and versatile sauce.

♥ High in vitamin C. Cleanses the palate.

Calendar

- Sow Feb–Jun every year for continual supply.
- Sow seeds once a month.
- Look out for carrot fly when the ground is dry.
- Harvest Mar–Sep.

	JAN	FEB	MAR	APR	MAY	JUN	JUL	AUG	SEP	OCT	NOV	DEC
Sowing/ planting time		☂	☂	■	■	■						
Harvest time				■	■	■	■	■	■			

Rosemary

Rosemary is a delight in the flower border and the herb garden for its wonderful blue or white flowers. The evergreen foliage is highly attractive, too. Like so many of our beautifully scented herbs, rosemary is Mediterranean and has a long history of medicinal and culinary use and many legends and stories about it.

Varieties

The most commonly grown rosemary is *Rosmarinus officinalis*, a blue-flowered shrub growing up to 1.2m/4ft tall with handsome narrow green glossy leaves, but there are many other varieties. For a more compact, low-growing type try the prostrate *R. officinalis* 'Prostratus'; for white flowers, *R. officinalis* 'Albiflorus'; and for a handsome, tall plant, 'Miss Jessopp's Upright' (purple flowers).

Growing tips

A sunny spot in well-drained soil is preferable, although some shade for part of the day is acceptable. This tall plant is ideal as a backdrop in a herb border and thrives next to a warm wall or fence.

Frost and cold winds can cut back the growth during the winter, so choose a sheltered spot. Prune after the main flush of flowers is over to prevent plants from becoming straggly, to encourage branching and to remove any diseased or frost-damaged shoots.

A few pests, such as leaf hoppers and frog hoppers, can cause problems during the summer, but are rarely troublesome enough to warrant spraying. Frog hoppers, which cause the distinctive cuckoo spit on the shoot tips, can be washed off with a strong jet of water.

Take 10cm/4in cuttings of rosemary in July or August and root in pots of 50:50 peat, or peat substitute, and sand. Hardwood cuttings, 23cm/9in long, can also be taken in September and rooted in slit trenches. Line the base of the trench with gritty sand and place the cuttings in to half their depth, 15cm/6in apart, before closing up again with your foot.

Container growing

Rosemary grows well in a container of John Innes No. 3 compost on a warm patio. Maintain watering during the summer and feed once a week with a liquid fertiliser.

In the kitchen

Hardy and prolific once mature, rosemary will fill your borders with a heady fragrance and provide a ready supply of aromatic needle-shaped leaves. Every cook knows the joys of rosemary with lamb, but it also enhances roasted vegetables, fish, potatoes and pulses. Whole sprigs can be added to slow-cooked dishes and left to infuse. Or pull the leaves away from the tough stalk and chop finely. Larger woody stalks can be used as attractive skewers. Simmer a few sprigs in a little water and sugar to create a fragrant syrup that can be served with poached fruit or drizzled over cakes.

♥ *Antibacterial and antifungal qualities. Add it to bath water.*

Calendar

- Plant purchased plants at any time, although spring planting allows them to become well established before winter.
- Plant Mar–Apr.
- Harvest all year.

	JAN	FEB	MAR	APR	MAY	JUN	JUL	AUG	SEP	OCT	NOV	DEC
Sowing/ planting time			■	■								
Harvest time	■	■	■	■	■	■	■	■	■	■	■	■

Sage

Salvia officinalis (common sage) and hybrids of it, such as 'Purpurascens' (the purple-leaved sage) and the variegated 'Tricolor' and 'Icterina' sages, are as popular for their decorative leaves as their use in the kitchen.

There are many 'fruit' scented sages with fragrances such as pineapple, blackcurrant, raspberry, peach and tangerine, which are generally less hardy so need a very sheltered spot in a border or on a patio.

Growing tips

Sages come from warmer southern Europe and need a sunny, sheltered, well-drained place in which to grow. If you have heavy soil, such as clay, dig in plenty of grit and well-rotted organic matter prior to planting.

Sage plants are short-lived and have a habit of becoming woody and straggly, so cutting shoots for the kitchen keeps them compact and younger for longer. It also delays flowering, which affects the quality of the leaves. Trim annually to maintain shape and vigour.

As plants tend to deteriorate over time, take a few cuttings each year to replace old stock. These root easily from tip cuttings – remove shoot tips about 5–7cm/2–3in long and push them into small pots or cell trays of multi-purpose compost mixed with a little grit or sand. Dipping the end of the cuttings in rooting hormone powder can help speed rooting, which can take as little as a month in the summer. It is also possible to grow plants from seed and these should be sown in the spring.

Container growing

The tender types of sage are best grown in pots to allow them to be moved to somewhere frost free in winter. As the prettiest are the most tender, they can make a lovely, fragrant display mixed with other sages or herbs.

Sage is used as a decorative plant for the border and for culinary use, and has been used medicinally for centuries. Our familiar garden sages are part of a large family that includes annuals, biennials and perennials. The sages that we usually enjoy in various recipes are mainly perennials that live for three years or longer and form attractive low shrubs.

Varieties

There are several popular sorts, all with strongly scented leaves and pretty heads of small flowers. The most commonly grown species is

In the kitchen

These powerful, thick chalky leaves add depth and a distinct muskiness to dishes. A strong herb and acquired taste, sage should be used sparingly and never raw. Infusing whole leaves into oils or stocks is a more subtle way to introduce sage's earthy flavour. Whole leaves are often fried in butter and used as an elegant, crispy garnish for meats. Traditionally, sage is used to complement fatty meats and as a stuffing for goose and pork. The essential oil of sage is known as sage clary and has been used to flavour wine and liqueurs.
♥ *Makes a soothing gargle for sore throats.*

Calendar

- Remove the flowers to maintain the quality of the leaves.
- Sow seeds Mar–Apr.
- Plant Apr–Sep.
- Harvest May–Sep.

	JAN	FEB	MAR	APR	MAY	JUN	JUL	AUG	SEP	OCT	NOV	DEC
Sowing/ planting time			🌱	🌱	■	■	■	■	■			
Harvest time						■	■	■	■			

Tarragon

Tarragon is a half hardy perennial that has a long history and is thought to have come to Britain in the Middle Ages. It became popular for its pungent leaves, perhaps as a way of covering up the taste of meats that were not fresh. Its name, *Artemisia dracunculus*, comes from the French for dragon as the roots coil like the mythical beast.

Varieties

There are two types, French tarragon and Russian tarragon, and the French one has the better flavour. However, you will have to buy a plant, as it does not produce viable seeds. Its Russian cousin produces a bigger crop of leaves, is hardier and so more likely to survive the winter – it can be grown from seed.

Growing tips

The seeds of Russian tarragon are sown in the spring but both types can be propagated, either by taking root cuttings or division. Plants may reach 1m/3ft 3in tall. Although perennial, it is best to treat Russian tarragon as an annual and to sow fresh seeds each year as plants soon

become straggly. However, if you wish to keep your plant through the winter, spread a thick mulch around the roots in the autumn to help insulate them from the cold.

In the case of French tarragon, take some cuttings in late summer and root them in time for the winter. Grow them on in a frost-free place and use them to replace the parent. Cuttings root very easily in a 50:50 mix of peat or coir and sharp sand, or you can dib them into cuttings compost in cell trays, one cutting per cell. To ensure success, give them a little heat in a propagator set to 15°C/60°F.

Outside, plant tarragon in a sunny border in well-drained, but water-retentive soil, digging in a little well-rotted organic matter to improve water-holding capacity. Cut regularly to keep the plants bushy and to avoid straggly growth.

Container growing

A small plant in a pot can be kept on a sunny windowsill during the winter to provide some out-of-season pickings. Tarragon will grow larger in a bigger container on the patio, filled with moisture-retentive but well-draining compost such as John Innes No. 3.

In the kitchen

Tarragon is a classic culinary herb with a sophisticated soft aniseed flavour. Because it is so pungent, it's important not to overdo it, just add a few leaves to taste. The soft leaves should be picked just before use, as they quickly lose their bite. Shred and use raw, or add towards the end of cooking for maximum impact. Tarragon's sweetness is great with tomatoes, chicken and eggs in particular. Traditionally, a French ingredient, it's often used to enhance a light soufflé or omelette. Pick leaves in midsummer to freeze.

♥ *An infusion of tarragon is said to aid sleep.*

Calendar

- Sow Russian tarragon Apr– May under cover.
- Take cuttings or divide the roots of either type in late summer.
- Harvest from garden May–Oct.

	JAN	FEB	MAR	APR	MAY	JUN	JUL	AUG	SEP	OCT	NOV	DEC
Sowing/ planting time				🌱	🌱							
Harvest time					■	■	■	■	■	■		

Thyme

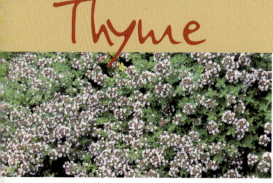

Brushing past sweetly perfumed thyme on a hot day has to be one of the delights of summer gardening. The leaves contain volatile oils that are more active in warm weather and on a still evening the fragrance is wonderful. If the climate in the UK is becoming warmer, drought-tolerant thymes could come into their own.

Varieties

There are over 400 species and around 100 varieties of thyme known to cultivation, all with subtle differences in scent and many with variegated leaves or delicate flowers in shades of white, pink and purple. *Thymus vulgaris* is most often used in cooking.

The various species vary in habit from mat-forming to upright in growth and at up to 30cm/12in tall, *T. vulgaris* is one of the taller ones. Others of note are the various varieties of *T. serphyllum* including 'Goldstream', with gold and green variegated leaves. Lemon thyme (*T. citriodorus*), another taller type, is widely available, as is *T. coccineus*, which grows in a red-flowered mat and is good for covering banks or growing in cracks in paving.

Growing tips

Although some thymes are native to the UK, many come from warmer climates such as the Mediterranean and are not completely hardy. However, most will thrive if given a warm, sunny spot, ideally in well-drained soil that is not too rich in nutrients. Mulch with a layer of gravel each year to retain a little moisture and keep water away from the crown of the plant in winter.

Sow seeds in potting compost in March, covering lightly, and keep in a warm place to germinate. Harden off and plant out when the seedlings are about 10cm/4in high and there's no danger of frost. You can also propagate by root division on three-year-old plants in April.

Pruning is important to keep the plants young and healthy. After flowering, trim back the old flower heads, shorten the stems and in spring lift up the edges of the clump and cut out any dead old shoots that tend to accumulate underneath.

Container growing

Thyme is ideal for growing in containers among other herbs, caring for them in exactly the same way. Keep them close to the back door for ease of picking and so that you can appreciate the scent they release.

In the kitchen

A favourite aromatic hardy herb that complements Mediterranean flavours. Either allow a whole sprig to infuse in a simmering casserole, or pull the small leaves away from the stalks, which can be discarded if old and woody. Stalks from a young, more tender plant can be used whole. Thyme retains its flavour during cooking, benefiting from a long, slow cook to allow the flavours to seep out – delicious in stews and stuffings. The woody sweetness is irresistible when added to soft onions, mushrooms or when roasting a chicken – tuck a knob of butter mixed with a handful of thyme leaves under the skin.

♥ An infusion of thyme makes a good mouthwash for sore gums.

Calendar

- Pick fresh at any time, but before flowering for preserving in oils or drying.
- Plant all year, avoiding hot, dry conditions. Sow Mar–Apr.
- Divide roots after 3 years.

	JAN	FEB	MAR	APR	MAY	JUN	JUL	AUG	SEP	OCT	NOV	DEC
Sowing/ planting time	■	■	■	■	■	■	■	■	■	■	■	■
Harvest time	■	■	■	■	■	■	■	■	■	■	■	■

how to grow your own

Fruit

Apples

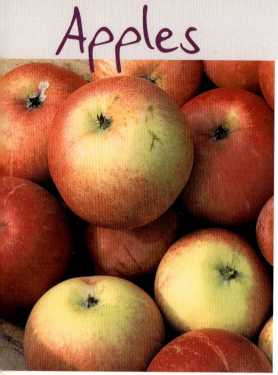

Apples are easy to grow, undemanding and, thanks to some excellent dwarfing rootstocks, it is possible to grow them in the smallest of gardens. If you have very little space, you can grow apples as cordons or espaliers against a fence, as step-over trees along the border edge or in tubs on a sunny patio.

Varieties

There are hundreds of varieties of apple to choose from, including culinary and dessert, and it is a good idea to go to an apple day event in the autumn and taste some to discover your preferences. Some types are better for containers than others, such as minarettes – varieties grown on a single main stem – or Ballerina apple trees, also small columnar trees. However, it is important to choose trees that have been grafted on to the correct rootstocks. Contrary to the usual advice, do not choose trees grafted on the very dwarfing rootstocks. Plants in pots are under stress and very dwarfing rootstocks can increase that stress. The semi-dwarfing rootstock M26 is a good choice for a tub. For best results you should grow two or three apple varieties to aid pollination.

Growing tips

Planting

Apple trees are very hardy, but the flowers are vulnerable to cold and will be damaged if the frost gets to them while they are waiting to be pollinated. It is important therefore to avoid planting in cold areas of the garden (frost

Fact file

- Apple seeds contain cyanide.
- Crab apples are decorative small trees and the ancestors of our cultivated varieties. The small, colourful apples make a delicious jelly.
- Evidence suggests that wild (crab) apples were eaten by Stone Age man.
- There are at least 5,000 named varieties of apple.
- Ripe apples should come away easily from the tree if gently lifted and twisted. If not, leave for a few more days. But try to pick them before they are blown off and become bruised.

pockets). A sunny spot is needed for good fruit set and ripening.

Apples prefer a free-draining soil with plenty of organic matter, such as garden compost or well-rotted manure, added when planting, but will often manage to produce a reasonable crop in poorer conditions.

When planting, make sure that the rootball is buried to the same depth as it was in the pot or in the nursery field – there is usually a soil mark on the stem.

Apples are nearly always grafted (the fruiting part is joined to the roots from another tree to control its growth; the knobble on the stem marking this point must be well above soil level after planting). When planting bare-rooted trees, dig a hole large enough to take the roots without bending them. You will need to provide a stake to prevent wind rock until the tree is established in its new growing position.

Growing on

Trained trees such as cordons and espaliers need hardly any pruning once established and are mainly pruned in August as the fruit is ripening; the side shoots are simply pruned back to three leaves. In the winter the main shoot is shortened to within three leaves of this season's growth. Ordinary bush-trained trees

In the kitchen

Apples are very versatile and have long been a favourite dessert ingredient, perhaps in part for their great keeping qualities. Varieties fall into two types: cooking and dessert. Cooking apples are acidic, tart and break down during cooking, while dessert apples are more crisp, sweet and sturdy.

Preparation and cooking: To prevent flesh turning brown, keep peeled and cut apples submerged in water with a squeeze of lemon juice. Enjoy in sweet, comforting crumbles, tarts and pies or as a sharp twist in savoury sauces and casseroles. Cooked apples partner rich meats and game perfectly and are sometimes enhanced with a touch of cinnamon.

Storage and freezing: Some varieties store better than others, and if you want apples to last through the winter, choose a late-maturing type. To store, wrap each apple individually in newspaper, place in a single layer in a box and store in a cool, dark place. Occasionally check for bad apples as they will taint and spoil the others.

Apples freeze well: peel, slice and open freeze them on a tray before putting in bags, or cook first and freeze when cold. Jams, jellies, juices and cider offer yet more ways to use apples well beyond the usual harvesting period.

♥ *High in vitamin A, some vitamin C and plenty of potassium – an important nutrient for cell function. Also high in antioxidants.*

need a little more attention, but will still produce a reasonable crop if left to their own devices. For best results, prune in the winter when the tree is dormant, removing dead wood, crossing branches and those in the middle of the tree which prevent air and light from entering.

One-year-old branches can be left alone, but shorten older shoots that are not wanted to replace old branches, to encourage fruiting spurs (stubby shoots on which the apples fruit) to form. Very long branches on the outside of the tree can be clipped back, but be careful not to get carried away, or you may remove some fruit buds. If unsure, leave alone.

Calendar

- Remove fruit in first year.
- A tree may lose some of a heavy crop naturally.
- Thin fruits to 10cm/4in apart for dessert apples, 15cm/6in for cookers Jun–Jul.

	JAN	FEB	MAR	APR	MAY	JUN	JUL	AUG	SEP	OCT	NOV	DEC
Planting time	■	■	■	■	■	■			■	■	■	■
Harvest time									■	■	■	

Container growing

When planted in pots, the trees can be moved around at will to avoid any problems – sheltered when flowering, open when fruiting. Plant trees in loam-based compost, such as a John Innes No. 2 or 3, as this retains water and nutrients better than loam-free compost and breaks down more slowly in the pot.

Any plant growing in a container must be watered regularly during dry spells and fed once a month from March to September with a liquid feed.

APPLE SAUCE

A sauce to add piquancy to savoury dishes. Omit the chilli for a sweet version.

4 large cooking apples, or 6 medium, peeled, cored and chopped
2 tbsp soft brown sugar
4 tbsp lemon juice
salt and freshly ground black pepper
1 hot fresh chilli, deseeded and finely chopped

1 Put the apples, sugar, lemon juice and seasoning into a heavy pan and add the chilli.
2 Cover the pan and cook very slowly, stirring occasionally, until the apples are soft and pulpy.

APPLE AND BLUEBERRY PIE

One of the superfoods, blueberries (see page 101) add a contrasting sweetness to the tart cooking apples in this pie, with a delicious result.

Serves 4–6

125g/4½oz blueberries
70–100g/2½–3½oz soft brown sugar
2 tbsp cornflour
grated zest and juice of ½ orange
pinch of ground cinnamon
375g/13oz pack ready-rolled shortcrust pastry
450g/1lb Bramley apples, peeled, cored and thickly sliced
beaten egg to glaze

1 Preheat the oven to 220°C/390°F/gas 7/fan oven 200°C and lightly grease a large baking sheet. Mix together the blueberries, sugar, cornflour, orange zest and juice and cinnamon.
2 Unfold the pastry and lay on the baking sheet. Pile the apples and blueberry mixture into the centre of the pastry. Roughly gather up the sides to enclose the fruit. Brush the pastry edges with the egg.
3 Bake the pie for 25–30 minutes until the pastry is golden and the apples and blueberries are tender. Transfer to a serving plate and allow to cool slightly.

Serve with: Custard or cream

Apricots are a favourite for drying and the nutrient-packed fruits make a great alternative to sugary sweets. However, the fresh fruit is delicious too and more widely available. But imported fruit that has travelled half way around the world often has little or no taste, so it's worth growing a modern variety in your garden.

Varieties

Fruit specialists now list several varieties of apricot (*Prunus armeniaca*) worth growing in the warmer south. As with their cousins the peach and nectarine, the trees are usually hardy; it is the blossom that suffers from the frost. However, new varieties such as 'Tomcot', a self-fertile French apricot bearing large fruit, and 'Goldcot', an early fruiting variety, are claimed to be very hardy and less sensitive to the cold. 'Flavourcot' is a Canadian variety that flowers late, avoiding the frosts.

Growing tips

Planting
Apricots have very similar requirements to peaches and nectarines (see page 113),

needing a sunny, sheltered site, avoiding frost pockets. The trees are supplied on plum rootstocks which help to control their growth – 'St Julien A' is a popular one as is 'Pixy', a very dwarfing rootstock.

If your garden is exposed, grow a tree as a fan, available ready-trained, and plant it in the shelter of a warm wall or fence. If you have a greenhouse, your tree can be grown inside for protection. Alternatively grow it in a pot.

Growing on
The planting and pruning of fans is the same as for peaches, and bush trees are pruned in the same way as plums (see page 117).

Pruning should be carried out in late winter/early spring and again in the summer to control growth, but it is best to keep it to a minimum. Dieback of the shoot tips is a common problem with apricots, simply clip them back to healthy wood when pruning.

Container growing

Apricots are ideal for growing in pots, as they can be moved when the weather demands it. For details on growing see Peaches on page 113.

Fact file
- Apricots originate from China and were popular with the Romans who grew them throughout their empire wherever conditions allowed.
- Today, Australia and Egypt grow large commercial crops for export.

Calendar
- Trees are self-fertile, but need help, especially under cover. Use a soft paintbrush to transfer pollen Feb–Mar.
- Plant trees in autumn or winter if you buy them bare-rooted.

	JAN	FEB	MAR	APR	MAY	JUN	JUL	AUG	SEP	OCT	NOV	DEC
Planting time	■									■	■	■
Harvest time								■	■			

Blackberries

A walk along any hedgerow in late summer will bring a tasty harvest of delicious berries from the brambles that weave their way through the undergrowth. If you love the taste of these wild berries, you will enjoy cultivated blackberries and their cousins the boysenberry, dewberry, loganberry, sunberry and many more.

Varieties

Choose your variety carefully as some are very vigorous – the long canes, often well armed with thorns, may reach up to 4.5m/15ft in a season. Many modern varieties are more compact, some growing to a comparatively modest 1.8m/6ft, such as blackberries 'Loch Ness' and 'Merton Thornless'. 'Helen' and 'Waldo' are both reasonably compact, thornless varieties, while if you have more space and thick gloves, 'Fantasia' might be for you.

Boysenberries are a little more vigorous, and the fruit resembles a long raspberry tasting more like the wild blackberry.

Loganberries are perhaps the best known of the hybrids and are a cross between raspberries and blackberries. The taste is sharp, so usually used for cooking. Thornless hybrids are available.

Growing tips

Planting

Blackberries and their hybrids like similar conditions to their cousins the raspberries (see page 119). Well-drained, but moisture-retentive soil is essential, although these tough plants will produce at least some fruit with only a bare minimum of attention.

Choose a site in the sun or semi-shade and provide adequate supports to tie the strong, vigorous canes to. The traditional way is to use strong wires, about 45cm/18in apart, stretched between posts, which creates an effective screen in the summer to shelter other crops, or an attractive barrier between vegetable plot and ornamental garden.

Your plants could last for 10–15 years, so it is worth taking time over soil preparation. Remove weeds, especially deep-rooted perennials and dig in plenty of well-rotted organic matter prior to planting. Be sure to add lots more around the roots each year in spring after applying a dressing of general fertiliser.

Plants need plenty of space to grow to avoid diseases. If a plant is likely to grow 1.8m/6ft in a season, this is the distance it should be spaced in the row.

Fact file

- Blackberries flower after the danger of sharp frosts have passed, so damage is usually negligible.
- Most varieties crop between July and September.
- Wild brambles are an important food source and place of shelter for wildlife during the winter.

BLACKBERRY VINEGAR

This fruity vinegar looks as good as it tastes, and can accompany virtually any meat as well as salads, vegetables and desserts. Recipes from the 18th century show that, mixed with a little water, it was used as a refreshing drink and with honey it provided relief for sore throats.

600ml/1pt by volume blackberries, hulled
600ml/1pt bottle of white wine vinegar
450g/1lb sugar
2 cinnamon sticks, broken (optional)
2 tsp each allspice berries and whole cloves (optional)

1 Mix the blackberries and vinegar together and leave covered in a bowl for 5–7 days at room temperature. Stir occasionally.
2 Strain through a muslin bag, or similar, into a stainless steel or enamelled saucepan. Discard the pulp.
3 Add the sugar to the liquid and heat gently, stirring with a wooden spoon until the sugar has dissolved. This may take an hour or so. If you wish to give your vinegar some additional spice, tie up the cinnamon, allspice berries and cloves in a muslin bag and pop into the pan when you add the sugar.
4 Bring to the boil slowly, stirring occasionally, then remove from the heat and keep covered while the liquid cools. Remove the spice bag if used.
5 Pour into sterilised bottles and seal with plastic caps or plastic-lined tops, as the vinegar will corrode metal, and store in a cool, dark place for up to 3 months.

Growing on

With very fast-growing plants, the canes can be woven around the wires so that they take up less space. Less vigorous varieties can be taken horizontally along the wires. In either case, separate the new growth, which will fruit next season, from the fruiting canes either by running it in a different direction along the wires, or by running them above the old canes. Tie in the canes regularly.

Once the fruit has been picked, remove the old growth completely at ground level, leaving the new canes to fruit next year. Some varieties produce too many canes, so cut away any

Calendar

- Plants may crop for up to 15 years, so buy good quality stock certified free from viruses, supplied by fruit specialists.
- Plant Nov–Mar.
- Harvest Jul–Sep.

	JAN	FEB	MAR	APR	MAY	JUN	JUL	AUG	SEP	OCT	NOV	DEC
Planting time	■	■	■								■	■
Harvest time							■	■	■			

In the kitchen

Formed from a fragile cluster of tiny berries that burst easily, blackberries need gentle handling. They are wonderful eaten raw, plucked fresh from the bush or dished up with a sprinkling of sugar and dash of cream.

Preparation and cooking: Wash the fruit only if necessary just before use and allow to dry thoroughly. Blackberries can be used in many favourite sweet dishes including pies, crumbles and ice creams as well as jams, jellies and preserves often mixed with other fruits, especially apples. Plump berries tint puddings with tantalising purple juice and autumnal sweetness. Bake in crumbles, tarts and sponges, or make into vibrant jams and sorbets. They can also be used in savoury dishes such as duck and game.

Storage and freezing: Refrigerate in a single layer so as not to crush the tender fruit. Open freeze on a tray and when frozen tip into a bag and return to the freezer. They are best brought back up to room temperature before serving, when the flavours are more mellow and ripe.

♥ *Rich in vitamins C and A and potassium, the quantities varying with each type.*

BAKED BLACKBERRY CHEESECAKE

Serves 4

100g/4oz butter
200g/7oz digestive biscuits, crushed
2 tbsp lemon juice
50g/2oz caster sugar
2 medium eggs
100g/4oz cream cheese
300ml/½pt double cream
250g/9oz blackberries
23cm/9in diameter deep, loose-bottom flan tin, greased

1 Preheat oven to 180°C/350°F/gas 4/fan oven 160°C. Melt the butter and mix with the crushed biscuits. Press the mixture evenly into the bottom of the dish with the back of a spoon. Bake for 10 minutes. Remove and cool.
2 Meanwhile, beat together the lemon juice and the caster sugar in a clean bowl until smooth. Beat in the eggs, one at a time, followed by the cream cheese and the cream and mix until smooth.
3 Arrange the blackberries on the cooled biscuit base and pour over the cream mixture. Bake for about one hour or until set in the middle. Cool completely before lifting out.
Serve with: More blackberries and cream.

excess for a better quality of crop. Aim to leave 20–25 canes on each plant. Birds will be deterred if you cover the plants with netting. However, cropping is usually so heavy at a time when there are plenty of other things for them to eat that this is seldom necessary.

Water well during the growing season, especially when the berries are swelling, and top up the mulch around the roots during dry spells in summer.

Container growing

Blackberries will not thrive in pots as they need a deep, moist root run, and the tendency for the compost to dry out and become warm in the sun does not suit them.

Blueberries

Blueberries were the first to be labelled a 'superfood' and, as well as being packed with goodness, they taste great and are easy to grow. The plants are attractive and compact enough to grow on the patio. They provide a visual treat all year: new leaves and flowers in spring, developing fruit in summer, and tinted leaves in autumn.

Varieties

'Bluecrop': The most popular variety and easy to obtain from fruit specialists.
'Colville': Ripens later and produces good yields of large berries.
'Earliblue': ripens earlier than most and produces a good crop of pale blue berries (pictured below).
'Herbert': Ripens in mid-August.

grow your crop in a raised bed filled with peaty compost or in pots using an ericaceous (lime-free) mixture.

Blueberries are self-fertile, but produce heavier yields if there is more than one plant. They need a sheltered, sunny position and must be kept well watered, using rainwater when possible.

Growing tips

Planting

Blueberries must grow in acid compost. So unless your garden has a naturally acid soil, such as peat or some sands, you will have to

Fact file

● 'Colville' is a blueberry named after American botanist Frederick Colville who hybridised some of the first varieties for cultivation.
● There are two types of blueberry – highbush and lowbush (also called bilberry). The latter is native to the UK. Highbush is the most popular with commercial growers for its ease of harvesting.

Calendar

● Buy bare-rooted plants in autumn and winter, or plants in pots.
● Plant bare-rooted Oct–Mar.
● Plant container-grown any time but avoid hot, dry spells.
● Harvest Jul–Aug.

	JAN	FEB	MAR	APR	MAY	JUN	JUL	AUG	SEP	OCT	NOV	DEC
Planting time	■	■	■							■	■	■
Harvest time							■	■				

In the kitchen

Intense silver-bloomed berries with a balanced flavour, blueberries add a burst of sweetness and a pleasant purple hue to many recipes. Use them to make delicious jams, pies, ice creams and jelly, not forgetting cheesecake!

Preparation and cooking: Blueberries grow in bunches and if you run these gently through your fingers when some of the berries appear ripe (completely blue over the whole surface), the ripe ones will come away, leaving those that need a little longer on the plant. After picking, leave them in a container with the lid off for a few hours before covering and placing in the fridge unwashed. This prevents a build-up of condensation, which can cause the berries to deteriorate.

Eat the berries raw or lightly poached in a little water, sugar and lemon juice. Use the softened fruit and syrup on top of cakes and desserts. They provide wonderful splashes of colour in muffins and pancakes. Just add the berries whole to the batter mix.

Storage and freezing: Store blueberries in a single layer, if possible, to prevent bruising and don't wash them until you are about to use them. You can open freeze the berries on a tray then seal in bags and return to the freezer for up to three months. They may lose their shape when defrosted.

♥ *High in vitamin C, antioxidants and dietary fibre.*

Growing on

Pruning is simple; there is none in the first two years after planting, then each year after that remove up to a third of the oldest shoots in the winter, cutting right down to soil level. Any dead, overcrowded or crossing shoots can be cut out at any time. Blueberries are very hardy, but the berries are irresistible to birds, so net plants as the fruit ripens.

Container growing

Blueberries are the ultimate fruit for growing in pots – on a sunny, sheltered patio or placed in the flower border. Plant in a pot about 5cm/2in larger than the root filled with ericaceous compost, mixed with some grit for drainage, and water well with rainwater during dry spells, keeping the compost moist, but not wet. Plants should thrive in the same pot for some years if well cared for; be prepared to rake away the surface of the soil each year and to replace with fresh material and some controlled-release fertiliser. However, in pots, the roots are vulnerable to winter frosts so ensure they stand in a sheltered spot, or wrap the pots in bubble wrap for extra insulation.

BLUEBERRY BREAKFAST DELIGHTS

Serves 3–4
600ml/1pt low fat crème fraîche
225g/8oz blueberries
a quality oat-based crunchy cereal, with dried strawberries

Using a large sundae or wine glass for each person, simply add alternate layers of crème fraîche, blueberries and cereal until full.
Serve with: Freshly brewed coffee and a croissant.

Cherries

This is one fruit that has everything going for it as far as the British climate is concerned. However, the flowers do not like the frost, so do not plant a cherry tree in an exposed site. With new dwarfing rootstocks, such as 'Colt' and, more recently, 'Gisela 5' and 'Tabel', trees of little more than 2m/6ft 6in are now possible.

Varieties

There are two main types, sweet cherries and sour or cooking varieties. Look out too for fan-trained trees and also 'family' trees with more than one variety grafted on to the same roots. The most familiar varieties are:

'Celeste': A self-fertile variety, and naturally compact.

'Merton Glory': Large yellow fruits flushed with orange; requires a pollination partner.

'Morello': A sour or culinary variety.

'Stella': A sweet cherry ripening in late July.

Fact file

● Cherries have been grown in the UK since the time of the Romans and are part of the rose family.
● Bacterial canker is the most common disease of cherries and causes dieback of the branches and the death of many old, weak trees.
● The US grows more cherries than any other country in the world, producing about 167.8m kg/370mlb of sweet cherries and around 136m kg/300mlb of sour cherries each year.

'Summer Sun': A modern red-fruited variety that can tolerate less warmth and shelter than other cherries.

Growing tips

Planting

Cherries prefer well-drained soil in the sun and shelter from late frosts. In colder gardens grow cherries as fan-trained trees and it is worth buying a ready-trained fan rather than doing it yourself. Plant in winter at a depth of 10cm/4in. Feed with a thick mulch of well-rotted garden compost or manure in the spring, which will also help to maintain the soil in good condition and retain water during the summer months. Apply a dressing of superphosphate (available from garden centres) every second year.

Plant fan-trained trees about 23cm/9in from the wall and angle towards the support.

Growing on

Pruning should be kept to a minimum by just removing crossing, damaged or dead branches. This must be done in the summer to limit the risk of bacterial canker and silver leaf entering the pruning cuts.

Cover the fruit with netting as it begins to ripen, to keep the birds at bay, and harvest as soon as the cherries are ripe, leaving the stalks attached.

In the kitchen

A beautiful and succulent British berry, so it's best to over indulge in the short season. There is little you can do to sweeten a sour, unripe cherry, so harvest when large, glossy and soft to the touch!

Preparation and cooking: When cooking cherries, pull them from their stalks and pit them first as the stones can be unpleasant and even dangerous if swallowed. Cherries are very versatile and can be used to make jams, pickles, pies, ice creams and fillings for pastries. They are a great accompaniment for ham, chicken, duck and even beef. Black pepper goes well with cherries, especially in combination with game, such as venison. Sour cherries are more tart, but with a good flavour. When cooked with adequate sugar, they too can be transformed into sweet pies, puddings and preserves.

Storage and freezing: Sweet cherries are best eaten fresh, although they do freeze well, either whole, or reduced down to a sticky sauce, which is delicious drizzled over desserts or duck. If freezing cherries, remove the stones first as they can taint the flavour of the fruit.

♥ *Cherries contain riboflavin with useful amounts of vitamin A and potassium.*

Container growing

Cherry trees can be grown in pots, which allows the flowers to be protected from frost during the spring. Aim for a pot at least 60cm/2ft in diameter and depth. They should not be kept in

CHERRY TIRAMISU

Mascarpone is delicious with so many things, but with cherries and a dash of strong coffee, it excels. It is ideal as a summer barbecue dessert.

Serves 4

200g/7oz sponge fingers
1 small cup espresso coffee
1 tbsp cherry brandy (optional)
200g/7oz ripe cherries, washed and pitted
150ml/¼pt double cream, lightly whipped
250g/9oz mascarpone cheese
50g/2oz icing sugar, sieved
100g/4oz dark chocolate, roughly chopped (optional)

1 Break the sponge fingers into a glass dish and pour over the espresso and brandy, if using. Place the cherries on top.
2 Blend the cream with the mascarpone and stir in the icing sugar and some small pieces of dark chocolate (optional).
3 Spoon the mascarpone mixture on to the cherries, smooth with a pallet knife and grate some more chocolate over the top. Decorate with a few more cherries.

a heated greenhouse or polytunnel, however, as like most fruit trees they need a period of cold to be able to fruit successfully.

Use a loam-based compost and top it up with 2.5–5cm/1–2in of fresh material each spring after removing the old surface layer. A sprinkling of controlled-release fertiliser will also help to keep the tree growing and fruiting well.

Keep the tree well watered particularly when the cherries are developing.

Calendar

- Plant container-grown trees any time but avoid hot, dry conditions.
- Plant bare-rooted trees in autumn and winter.
- Support the young tree until the roots are established.

	JAN	FEB	MAR	APR	MAY	JUN	JUL	AUG	SEP	OCT	NOV	DEC
Planting time	■	■									■	■
Harvest time						■	■	■				

Red, white and blackcurrants, simple to grow, thrive in all parts of the UK and require very little attention from the gardener. White and redcurrants can be trained into various forms, such as cordons. They can also be trained into fans and espaliers. Blackcurrants are generally grown as bushes. All are self-fertile.

Varieties

Currants are prone to a number of pests and diseases, so look for modern resistant varieties.
'Ben Hope': Blackcurrant resistant to big bud mite – tiny creatures which cause the buds to swell – and the reversion virus.
'Jonkheer Van Tets': Heavy yielding redcurrant, an award-winning early variety.
'White Versailles': A vigorous, heavy cropping white currant.

The jostaberry is a cross between a blackcurrant and gooseberry and is resistant to many of the problems to which blackcurrants are prone. The berries are black, larger than

blackcurrants and the bushes are very high yielding. Prune as you would for blackcurrants.

Growing tips

Planting

Like most fruits, currants need a free-draining but moisture-retentive soil in a position that gets some sunshine. However, red and white currants are happy to grow in partial shade and cooler conditions and are suitable therefore for north-facing walls and gardens, where few other fruits will thrive. Blackcurrants will crop better in a sunny spot.

With all three types, dig in plenty of well-rotted organic matter prior to planting and each spring give the plants a feed with sulphate of potash at the rate of 50g per sq.m/2oz per sq yd, before topping up the mulch again.

Fact file

- Although closely related, redcurrants and white currants (*Ribes sativum, R. arubrum*) are a different species to blackcurrants (*R. nigra*). Blackcurrants hail from northern Europe and Asia, red and white from Western Europe.
- Redcurrants and white currants are mainly used in cooked dishes or as a garnish since they are quite sour in comparison with sugar-rich blackcurrants.

Calendar

- Plant during the dormant season Nov–Mar; mulch well in spring.
- Will grow on heavy soils but need some shelter from cold winds in early season.

	JAN	FEB	MAR	APR	MAY	JUN	JUL	AUG	SEP	OCT	NOV	DEC
Planting time	■	■	■								■	■
Harvest time						■	■	■				

Growing on

Red and white currants usually grow on a single short stem, although stool-type plants (where shoots emerge from below ground level with no main stem) are common. Prune in winter from November to March, when the bushes are dormant, and again during the summer. In winter, cut the new main shoots produced during the last growing season back by half and the side shoots to about 5cm/2in and cut out any diseased or badly angled or crossing shoots completely. In late June to July, cut back all the side shoots to four or five leaves from the base.

Cordons are easy to prune; cut back the leading shoot to one bud above last season's growth in late winter and trim all the side shoots back to four or five leaves in summer, as above.

Prune blackcurrants, which grow as a stool, in winter, although it is easier to cut out about a quarter

In the kitchen

Tiny translucent fruit, with a spicy aroma reminiscent of grapes, the red, white and black varieties of currant are all bursting with vitamin C.
Preparation and cooking: Pull away the coarse top of the currant; it is a shrivelled remnant of the flower and should be removed before using. Make the currants into juice or add to other fruit juices; add to summer tarts, pies and puddings and, as they contain high levels of pectin – the natural setting agent in fruit – they make great jellies and jams. The sweet acidity of currants makes them a fine accompaniment to lamb and game, usually as a jelly.
Storage and freezing: Currants store very well. They are firm and will not deteriorate or wither in the fridge or freezer. All currants can be preserved, either by open freezing whole on trays, then bagging them up and returning to the freezer, or by crushing them with sugar and freezing in plastic boxes or bags.
♥ *Blackcurrants are high in vitamin C and anthocyanins – more even than blueberries.*

WARMING WINTER PUDDING

This delicious pudding is very satisfying after a hard day in the garden spent digging.
Serves 6
225g/8oz self-raising flour
100g/4oz shredded suet
pinch of bicarbonate of soda
salt
250ml/8fl oz water plus 1 tbsp for the fruit
450g/1lb frozen blackcurrants (or 225g/8oz blackcurrant jam), thawed
200g/7oz sugar
1.2 litre/2pt pudding basin, greased

1 Mix the flour and suet with the bicarbonate of soda and a pinch of salt. Stir in the water slowly to form a soft dough. Roll out into a thin layer and use two-thirds of it to line the pudding basin. Trim the excess.
2 Fill with the fruit (or jam), sugar and 1 tbsp water. Cut the left-over dough into a lid to fit the basin, moisten the edges around the rim, place the lid on top and seal the edges.
3 Cover the pudding with greaseproof paper, pleated once for expansion and tied on with string, and steam for up to 3 hours. Or give it 8 minutes in a microwave oven on full power (750w oven). Allow to stand for a few minutes.
Serve with: Thick, creamy custard and, if you like, hot blackcurrant jam.

of the oldest shoots completely at harvest time, or just afterwards. Diseased and weak shoots can be taken out then, too. In this way no shoot will remain that is more than four years old.

Container growing

It is possible to grow redcurrants and white currants in pots at least for the first three or four years, although they are generally happier in the garden, where they can keep their roots in cool, moist soil. If you do attempt to grow them in containers, ensure that the soil is kept moist, but not wet, at all times.

Figs

You don't need to live in the Mediterranean to enjoy the fig's wonderful sweet flesh as it can grow very well in many areas of the UK. Fig trees are surprisingly hardy – in most seasons, only some shoot tips or young fruits, which form in leaf joints at the end of the branches, are killed by frost, causing the plant no long-term damage.

Varieties

Over the many centuries that figs have been cultivated, a large number of varieties have been bred, but not all are suitable for our climate or readily available from nurseries, although if you have a greenhouse the choice is much greater. Try the old favourites 'Brown Turkey' and 'White Marseilles', both of which are reliable and easy to get from garden centres or fruit specialists.

For the greenhouse, 'Rouge de Bordeaux' is a pale green fig with a purple flush and sweet red flesh.

Fact file

● The fig is not a fruit at all, but a special structure called a syconium. The flowers are on the inside and not seen until the fig is cut open.

● In their native southwest Asia and eastern Mediterranean, figs are pollinated by tiny wasps that enter the 'fruit' through the opening at the base to lay their eggs. Since there are no fig wasps in the UK, our figs don't produce seeds.

Growing tips

Planting

Fig trees are very vigorous and it is often recommended that they be planted into a 'container' with paving slab sides or old bricks, to restrict the roots. However, this is only necessary if the conditions are likely to give rise to excessive growth – if the soil is deep and rich. A dry soil, low in nutrients, will have the same curtailing effect. It is best, therefore, not to add compost or manure to the soil prior to planting, but simply to plant in a hole a little larger than the rootball and firm in well.

Figs do not like to have their feet wet for long periods in heavy soils, so with clay, break up the base of the hole with a fork prior to planting and add some grit to both the hole and the soil used to back fill around the roots.

Growing on

If your plant has just one stem, prune it back to a healthy bud to encourage branching. Otherwise, pruning should be carried out in March, to shape the plant, cut out overcrowded, thin and crossing branches and to remove the tips of the young shoots. In June to July, pinch out the tips of all the new growth to encourage fruits to form.

When the leaves drop, remove all the developing figs that are larger than the nail on

FIG TARTE TATIN

This deliciously sweet treat offers a simple way to use up some of those excess figs.

Serves 4–6

6 large figs, stalks removed
25g/1oz butter
25g/1oz caster sugar
250g/9oz ready-rolled puff pastry
shallow ovenproof dish 20cm/8in in diameter, greased

1 Preheat the oven to 200°C/400°F/gas 6/fan oven 180°C. Cut the figs into quarters.
2 Melt the butter in a pan and add the figs and the sugar. Cook for 6–7 minutes until slightly brown and caramelised.
3 Place the figs in the greased shallow ovenproof dish and top with the rolled pastry, tucking in the sides and pricking all over with a fork.
4 Bake for 20–25 minutes until crisp and golden. Remove from the oven and allow to cool for a few minutes.
5 To serve, loosen the tart around the edges with a knife, place a plate upside down over the pastry and invert, removing the dish.

Serve with: Cream.

Container growing

Figs can be grown in large containers and this is a good way to keep them in check. Plant in John Innes No. 3 compost and maintain watering during the summer months. A sunny, sheltered spot is best and in the winter the extra protection that comes from a warm wall or a few layers of fleece should increase the harvest the following year. Feed pot-grown plants every week from April to September with a half-strength solution of tomato fertiliser.

In the kitchen

Figs are best eaten just over-ripe when fragrant, sweet and soft to the touch.

Preparation and cooking: It is important to handle figs with care – the delicate skins bruise easily, which will taint and spoil the fruit. Figs are suitable for making into jam and chutney, cakes, puddings and ice cream. They can also be eaten raw and fresh in salads, roasted whole in foil parcels or poached in a sticky red wine syrup. Fresh figs are sumptuous with sweet, dry-cured hams and are often paired together in Mediterranean cuisine.

Storage and freezing: To preserve figs, they can be dried in an airing cupboard and will take about a week to dry properly; alternatively, a special food drier can be used.

♥ High in vitamin A and potassium. Also a high energy food, as figs are nearly half sugar.

your little finger as these won't survive the winter and will reduce the crop next year.

Harvest your figs as soon as they become soft as they will quickly become over-ripe or the birds, or wasps, will get them first!

Calendar

- Greenhouse-grown plants may produce two crops each year.
- Plants can be grown in pots and moved inside for the winter.
- Plant Nov–Mar.
- Harvest Aug–Sep.

	JAN	FEB	MAR	APR	MAY	JUN	JUL	AUG	SEP	OCT	NOV	DEC
Planting time	■	■	■								■	■
Harvest time								■	■			

Gooseberries

Native to Europe, gooseberries have been grown in the UK for centuries. Extremely hardy, they only need protection from birds. However, some varieties are quite sour and difficult to work with as they are covered with sharp thorns. Getting to grips with pruning is important for the best crops but they will crop even when neglected.

Varieties

Many types of gooseberry have been bred and there are competitions to find the largest fruit. The biggest has been reported to be as large as a goose egg and weighed over 50g/2oz.

Gooseberries come in red, yellow, green and white-berried varieties, but the most common are either red or green.

'Invicta': A culinary, green fruit with good resistance to American gooseberry mildew, a common disease.

'Pax' and 'Rokula': Modern, heavy cropping, red dessert varieties with good disease resistance to replace 'Whinham's Industry'.

Fact file

- Gooseberries can be propagated by taking long shoots from healthy plants in the winter and burying them to half their depth in trenches in a sheltered spot, where they can be left undisturbed until rooted.
- Gooseberry juice was used in the 16th century to reduce fevers.
- Watering evenly is important to prevent the fruit from splitting should it receive a sudden downpour after a dry spell.

Growing tips

Planting

Gooseberries prefer a deep, moist soil, which is reasonably fertile, so dig in plenty of well-rotted manure or garden compost prior to planting. Each spring, scatter 25–50g/1–2oz of fertiliser, such as Growmore, or pelleted chicken manure around the roots as well as a layer of organic matter.

Choose a sunny site and, since gooseberries flower and fruit earlier than any other soft fruit, avoid planting in a frost pocket.

Growing on

Regular pruning is important to give the best yields. This is done in two stages in the winter and summer. Prune to maintain an open, vase-shape to the bush, to allow air and light to reach the centre of the plant.

Between October and March, cut back the shoots produced in the previous season by about half, and cut the side shoots arising from the remaining stems to 5cm/2in to a point just above an outward-facing bud. Cut out old, diseased or damaged wood at the same time and shorten branches on lax varieties growing close to the ground, to prevent the fruit from trailing on the soil. In late June, cut back the side

Calendar

- Space bushes 1.2m/4ft apart.
- Cordons 45cm/18in apart.
- Plant Oct–Mar.
- Harvest late Jun–late Aug.
- Watch out for caterpillars of gooseberry sawfly early summer.

	JAN	FEB	MAR	APR	MAY	JUN	JUL	AUG	SEP	OCT	NOV	DEC
Planting time	■	■	■							■	■	■
Harvest time							■	■				

In the kitchen

These large veiny, hairy berries are a traditional taste of a British summer. Cooked with plenty of sugar, gooseberries are delicious in pies and jams. The dessert varieties can be sweet if they get enough sun to ripen the berries fully.

Preparation and cooking: Plump, green, sour and slightly under ripe berries are best for cooking with. Later-season, red-blushed berries can be eaten raw with a sprinkling of sugar. Easy to prepare and cook, top and tail with scissors and wash thoroughly. Poach with plenty of sugar and a splash of water. The pulp can then be used in crumbles, ice creams or in the famous creamy, frothy fool. Gooseberries go well with oily fish such as mackerel and they can be used to make jams, preserves and wine. Their flavour complements other fruits such as redcurrants, and elderflowers are often mixed with them to enhance flavour. The fruit sets well in chutneys and preserves – stew until very soft, as you don't want whole fruit in gooseberry jam.

Storage and freezing: Picked young and firm, gooseberries freeze well whole or, when ripe, lightly cooked and sweetened, or as a purée. Open freeze under ripe berries in a single layer on a tray, pour into bags and return them to the freezer.

♥ *Contain useful amounts of vitamin C, folate and potassium.*

SPICY GOOSEBERRY CHUTNEY

450g/1lb gooseberries, trimmed
350g/12oz seedless raisins or chopped dates
225g/8oz onion, finely chopped
50g/2oz soft brown sugar
600ml/1pt cider vinegar
2 tsp mixed pickling spice in a muslin bag
salt

1 Stir all the ingredients together in a preserving pan and add the spice bag. Leave covered overnight.
2 Remove the lid and heat gently, stirring until the sugar has dissolved.
3 Boil gently for a few minutes, then reduce to a simmer, stirring occasionally. Watch the pan carefully and after about 20 minutes when the liquid has gone and the chutney is soft, remove from the heat. If the chutney has begun to stick to the pan add a little more vinegar.
4 Allow to cool and remove the bag of spice before spooning the chutney into clean, sterilised jars. Leave for a few weeks to mature.

shoots to five leaves from their base to remove much of the soft growth, which is likely to become infected with mildew.

Gooseberries can also be grown as cordons and should be pruned in the same way as currants (see page 106). In spring, look out for signs of green caterpillars with black spots. These are the caterpillars of the gooseberry

sawfly, which can quickly strip the leaves from the whole plant. Pick them off or spray with a suitable insecticide.

When the fruit softens slightly, it is ready to pick.

Container growing

Gooseberries generally do best when planted in open soil. However, they do make good standards (bush plants grown on a long stem) and these can be grown in the border as a decorative plant or in a large tub on the patio. It is essential to provide plenty of water and food throughout the growing season.

When growing in pots, use a loam-based compost such as John Innes No. 3 as this will hold water well and being heavier than peat-based compost will provide more stability.

Grapes

rape vines were introduced to the UK by the Romans. In more recent times, the British climate has only been suitable for growing crops reliably in greenhouses but with milder winters, it is becoming more of a practical proposition to grow grapes outside across Britain, although you need to choose a suitable variety.

Varieties

Not only do you have the choice between dessert and wine grapes, but there are indoor and outdoor varieties, as well as black or white-berried vines.

OUTDOOR PLANTING
'Boskoop Glory': A delicious black dessert or wine grape.
'Madeleine Angevine': A heavy cropping white wine grape.
'Siegerrebe': A white dual-purpose variety.
Strawberry grape: A dessert type.

INDOOR PLANTING
'Black Hamburgh': One of the best-known dessert varieties and one of the most popular for growing in a greenhouse.
'Buckland Sweetwater': Compact and sweet-berried.
'Thompson's Seedless': Vigorous white dessert variety.

Growing tips

It is still important, especially when growing dessert grapes, to choose a variety which is best suited to the climate in your region, in order to benefit from a good, sweet crop of grapes.

The key to good grapes is sun, sun, sun. This is because sunlight is essential if the fruit is to produce the sugar necessary to make the berries sweet. Vines must, therefore, be planted in a sunny south-facing, sheltered spot, such as against a warm wall, and be supported by strong wires. The strawberry grape is a good choice for planting outdoors in such a spot.

If you don't have these requirements consider growing an indoor variety in a cold greenhouse, conservatory or well-ventilated polytunnel.

Planting

The soil should be well drained and reasonably deep and fertile. Dig in plenty of well-rotted garden compost or manure at least a month prior to planting and fork over the base of the hole to improve drainage. Scatter some general-purpose fertiliser or pelleted chicken manure over the planting area.

Fact file
- Grapes have been cultivated for thousands of years, perhaps for as long as 8,000 years. The ancient Egyptians were cultivating them in 2000 bc.
- One good vine should give you around 6.8 kg/ 15lb of fruit.
- The Victorians were expert in the art of grape growing in heated greenhouses and many of the original greenhouses, and even some of the vines, can still be seen.

Calendar
- Plant and prune Nov–Feb when dormant to reduce stress.
- Pruning during winter reduces loss of sap from the pruning cuts.
- Harvest Sep–Oct.

	JAN	FEB	MAR	APR	MAY	JUN	JUL	AUG	SEP	OCT	NOV	DEC
Planting time	■	■									■	■
Harvest time									■	■		

In the kitchen

A ripe, sun-warmed grape can be delicious straight off the vine, but native fruit from warmer climes can often be very acidic when grown in cooler temperatures. Grapes make great juices and, of course, wine.

Preparation and cooking: Sharp grapes can be cooked until caramelised and sweet. Roast them with poultry or game, or bake in tarts and crumbles. They can also be used to make jellies or eaten at any time as a healthy, low calorie snack. Pair with cheese or throw into salads; cook, freeze or ferment to make the most of your crop.

Storage and freezing: To maintain plumpness and flavour, store unwashed on the stalk, refrigerated in an airtight container. Pluck and rinse the fruit then spread them on a tea towel to dry. Open-freeze on trays and seal in bags, to be enjoyed as cooling ice-grape sweets. Frozen grapes are also easier to peel.

♥ *Contain antioxidants and high in vitamin C and potassium. An energy food due to high sugar levels.*

Growing on

To keep your vine under control, it is best to grow it as a cordon (single straight main stem or rod) or multiple cordon (several straight main stems arising from the same plant). These main stems arise from horizontal branches running along the bottom wire and are kept as a permanent framework on which the fruiting side shoots are formed.

As the side shoots grow, train them out either side of the main rods and once a bunch begins to form, pinch back the shoot to two leaves from the bunch, to concentrate the plant's energy on the fruit.

During the winter, cut back the tip of the rod by half of the growth made in the previous year and, as the rods age, replace them with other suitably placed rods which have formed on the horizontal branches.

With dessert grapes, if the bunches have set a large number of berries, you may need to thin them out to improve the size and quality of the remainder. This must be done in several stages and begins when the fruit is the size of a pea until there is 1cm/½in between the fully grown berries.

Although grapes like to grow in well-drained soil, watering during the summer is important to maintain even moisture levels and to help prevent the fruit from splitting and getting mildew. This is why traditionally, the roots of greenhouse grapes were planted outside the greenhouse, with the stem running underneath the wall and into the structure.

Once the grapes are soft and sweet, you can begin harvesting. Snip the bunch off the stem by cutting it half an inch or so either side of the main stalk. Handled carefully, your grapes may store for six to eight weeks if kept cool with the cut end in water.

Container growing

Grapevines can be grown very successfully in a large pot or tub filled with a loam-based John Innes compost, but they do need additional care. Place the pot on a sunny, sheltered patio during the summer, but, if possible, bring the plant indoors into an unheated greenhouse or polytunnel for the winter where it will be sheltered from cold winds and heavy frosts.

Keep the vine reasonably moist during the growing season and feed regularly with a high potash tomato food from April to September.

Pruning is different, too, and rather than relying on a system of permanent rods, cut all growth back to within a bud during the dormant season to maintain a tight head.

CHEESECAKE-STYLE GRAPE DESSERT

This light, refreshing and low-fat dessert is just the thing to clear the palate after a spicy main course.

Serves 4

1 packet of lemon jelly
200g/7oz ricotta cheese
2 tbsp caster sugar
1 tbsp grated lemon zest
medium bunch large seedless red grapes
½ tsp vanilla essence
mint leaves to garnish (optional)

1 Dissolve half the packet of jelly according to the instructions. Allow to cool slightly before blending with the ricotta, sugar and lemon zest. Half fill small glass dishes with the mixture and chill until almost set.
2 Meanwhile dissolve the remaining jelly in a bowl and chill until it has almost set.
3 Cut the grapes in half and arrange on top of the mixture in the dishes to represent bunches of grapes. Use mint leaves for the vine leaves.
4 Spoon the remaining soft jelly carefully over the top and place in the fridge to set.

Serve with: A scoop of ice cream, if desired.

Peaches

Although peaches can be grown outdoors in milder or more sheltered areas of the UK, their success is reliant on the weather. In a mild year, peaches can crop well, but in a cold, wet season expect a low yield. Nectarines, with their smooth skins, are even less reliable and ideally require a greenhouse, polytunnel or conservatory.

Varieties

Some varieties of peach are better suited to the British climate than others. The most reliable are:

'Peregrine' and 'Rochester': These can be grown in the open in warm or sheltered areas, especially when grown as fans against a warm wall.

Nectarines are suitable only for very favoured areas, try:

'Early Rivers' and 'Lord Napier': These are the ones most often seen in catalogues.

Growing tips

Planting

Choose a site which is both sheltered and sunny on free-draining soil, which holds plenty of moisture during the summer. Improve dry soils by digging in well-rotted garden compost or manure prior to planting, either outside or in the greenhouse border.

If growing as a fan, buy a three-year-old tree that has already been partly trained. Before planting, fix some strong wires to the wall with vine eyes at 45cm/18in intervals to support the framework of branches as they grow.

Growing on

Pruning should not be done in the winter, but in late spring or early summer when the sap rises as this helps to prevent bacterial canker and silver leaf.

Bushes are trained in much the same way as plum trees (see page 117), but for fans cut back any branches growing away from the wall or into it, then thin the side shoots on each branch by pinching off every other one. In May, cut back the growth from the remaining side shoots to five or six leaves. Finally, after fruiting cut back to the lowest shoot on each side branch,

removing all but the lowest shoot. This is the replacement shoot – the one on which fruit will develop next season.

If the crop is heavy, the fruits may require thinning in stages until they are 20cm/8in apart, to ensure good size and quality.

Give your tree a dressing of fertiliser, such as Growmore, or pelleted chicken manure in the spring before mulching with well-rotted garden compost, and cover ripening fruit to deter wasps and birds.

Container growing

Peaches are ideal for growing in pots since they can be moved indoors into a frost-free greenhouse, conservatory or polytunnel from February when flowering, then placed in a sheltered spot outside once the frosts are over.

As with many fruit trees, peaches and

Fact file

- Peaches, nectarines and apricots (see page 97) are closely related. They belong to the Prunus family, which includes cherries and plums.
- Although the flowers are easily damaged by frost, the trees are very hardy. In fact peaches need a period of cold to bring about winter dormancy and to fruit well the following year.
- Peaches originate from China, but were thought by many in ancient times to have come from Persia, hence the botanical name of *Prunus persica*.

nectarines are usually grafted onto rootstocks to control their growth. To grow peaches in a pot, look for a tree grafted on to St Julian A or Pixy.

Grow in a large 38–45cm/15–18in pot

FLOGNARDE WITH PEACHES

This recipe also works well with apricots, plums or pears.

Serves 8

8 peaches, halved and stoned
25g/1oz butter
6 sticks of angelica
100g/4oz sugar plus sugar for sprinkling
grated zest of lemon
4 tbsp brandy or sweet white wine
50g/2oz plain flour, sifted
250ml/8fl oz single cream
3 eggs, beaten

1 Preheat the oven to 200°C/390°F/gas 6/fan oven 180°C. Cut each peach half into three slices.

2 Heat the butter, angelica and 75g/3oz of the sugar in a large frying pan, then add the fruit and cook slowly for 8–10 minutes. Remove from the heat and stir in the lemon zest and brandy or wine and leave to cool.

3 Strain, reserving the juices, and arrange the cooked fruit in greased individual ramekin dishes or one large dish.

4 Combine the flour, cream, remaining sugar, eggs and juices from the cooked fruit in a bowl with a hand mixer until blended, and pour over the fruit. Sprinkle more sugar on top.

5 Bake for 25–30 minutes until browned and risen.

Serve with: Single cream.

In the kitchen

Nothing beats the sensual juicy flesh of a ripe, sun-kissed peach. Ripen on the tree and pluck when the fruit is warm, heavy and juicy. Take great care when picking peaches and nectarines as they bruise very easily. Lift and twist gently and if the fruit does not come away easily, leave it for a few more days.

Preparation and cooking: Stone, peel and cut into quarters for desserts. Use raw, or enhance the flavour by baking or poaching in caramelised syrup. The classic Peach Melba made with fresh ripe fruit is a revelation. Simmer halves in sugar, water, vanilla and lemon juice and serve with the sticky sauce and cream. Halves are delicious doused in your favourite liqueur and jarred and stored or shared as gifts. Peaches and nectarines make wonderful jams, pies, liqueurs and ice creams. They can be juiced and are sometimes used in chutney and as an accompaniment for roast pork.

Storage and freezing: If harvested under ripe, allow the fruit to soften on a sunny windowsill but don't keep in the fridge, as they will remain hard, bland and floury. Cooked peach and nectarine dishes can be frozen, otherwise eat straight from the tree.

♥ *High in vitamins C and A, potassium and niacin (vitamin B3) and a little fibre.*

filled with John Innes No. 3 compost and keep on a sunny, sheltered patio during the summer.

In the autumn move the tree into a greenhouse or, if this is not possible, a shed, garage or simply close to the house wall where it will be sheltered from the worst of the winter wind. In spring, protect the blossom from frost with horticultural fleece if the tree cannot be taken under cover.

Although both peaches and nectarines are self-fertile, they blossom when few insects are on the wing to pollinate them, so to be sure, pollinate them yourself with a soft brush. Each spring, add a new layer of fresh compost to the top of the pot and feed every 14 days, as the fruit is developing, with a high potash tomato food.

Calendar

● The dates on the chart relate to bare-rooted trees; plant container-grown plants any time, preferably in autumn.
● Plant Oct–Mar.
● Harvest mid Jul–mid Sep.

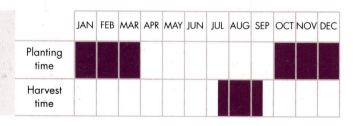

	JAN	FEB	MAR	APR	MAY	JUN	JUL	AUG	SEP	OCT	NOV	DEC
Planting time	■	■	■							■	■	■
Harvest time							■	■	■			

Although pears are not the easiest fruit to grow, due to their susceptibility to frosts at blossom time, given the right conditions, they will thrive and crop heavily, but if you live in the north of the UK or have an exposed garden, it is best to grow pears as a fan or cordon against a warm south or west-facing wall or fence.

Varieties

Pears have been grown for many centuries and as a result a large number of varieties have been bred. The main groups are culinary (cooking) and dessert (eating), the latter being a better choice for growing in the garden. Perry pears are grown for making a fine alcoholic drink and tonic, but are not generally suitable for smaller gardens.

'Beth': An early dessert pear cropping in September. Not self-fertile.

'Concorde': A late dessert variety cropping in October/November.

'Conference': The most popular dessert variety and partly self-fertile.

'Williams' Bon Chretien': Another dessert variety with a great flavour. Crops in September, but does not store well. Both 'Beth' and 'Conference' will pollinate it.

Growing tips

Planting

Follow the planting and training advice given for apples (see page 95) and you won't go far wrong. However, pears are fussier than apples when it comes to site. The much earlier flowering means that it is important to find a sheltered spot, especially when growing bush trees in the open. If this is not possible, stick to trained types such as cordons, fans and espaliers, which can be grown against a warm wall.

Pears do have the advantage of tolerating heavier soils than apples, but dislike chalky conditions. Choose a reasonably free-draining, moisture-retentive soil and when planting make sure that the graft union is at least 23cm/5in above the surface to prevent the fruiting wood from rooting into the soil and bypassing the parent rootstock.

Growing on

When the blossom appears, keep some horticultural fleece handy to protect the flowers from frost – wall-trained trees can sometimes be covered completely with a sheet suspended over the top, but be sure to uncover during the day when insects are interested.

Mulch each year in the spring after applying a general fertiliser. If you have a heavy crop, it may be necessary to thin the fruit to improve the quality.

Not many varieties are self-fertile, so if you have little space, train 'Conference' as a space-saving espalier along a fence or wall.

Harvesting

Pears should be harvested when nearly ripe, since if left to become over ripe they won't store well. Most tend to turn from a very acid green

Fact file

- Pears are closely related to apples, both belonging to the *Malus* family.
- Pears are long-lived trees, often still cropping well at 50 years or more, but they can take 4–8 years to come into fruit.
- Look out for pear midge, which can cause the young fruits to turn black before they reach maturity.
- 'Williams' Bon Cretien' is a popular dessert pear and is hardy enough to be grown in colder northern areas.

TRADITIONAL POACHED PEARS

Serves 4

8 pears, without blemishes
750ml/1¼pts (approx) red wine or port
zest and juice of 1 orange
zest and juice of 1 lemon
100g/4oz sugar
1 vanilla pod
4 whole cloves

1 Peel the pears, leaving them whole and retaining the stalks, and carefully cut out the core from the base. Place the pears upright in a large saucepan and pour over enough wine or port to cover them. The wine can be diluted with a little water if necessary. Add the zest and juice of the orange and lemon plus the sugar, vanilla and cloves.

2 Cover the saucepan and simmer for 15–30 minutes, checking the pears frequently by lifting out with a slotted spoon and pushing a paring knife into the base. The pears should be soft, but able to retain their shape once cooked. Cooking time will vary depending on the variety and ripeness of the pears.

3 Lift out of the pan and place in a serving dish. Pour over the liquid and allow to cool.

Serve with: Cornish vanilla ice cream.

In the kitchen

The perfect fruit for the English garden, as versatile as the apple but more complex.

Preparation and cooking: When soft, sweet and ungritty, pears are the perfect foil for any sharp blue cheese. This, combined with bitter leaves and walnuts, can create a noteworthy salad. Late season dessert pears, such as 'Concorde', cook well and are especially good for desserts. Divine when drizzled with dark chocolate, in tarts or simmered in sweetened red wine. There are numerous delicious recipes that use pears and they can often be a substitute for apples in pies, flans or for baking or making juices, purées and chutney – they can even be barbecued.

Storage and freezing: A well-stored harvest will bring joy to the winter kitchen. Keep pears in a cool, dark and dry place (see Harvesting) or bottle, poached in syrup. Pears can also be frozen in the same way as plums (see page 118). One of the easiest ways to preserve them is by pickling in a boiled solution of white distilled vinegar and sugar to which you can add spices such as cinnamon, allspice, ginger and cloves, to taste.

♥ *Rich in potassium, vitamin C and fibre. Pears also contain useful amounts of calcium.*

to a slightly lighter hue when ready for picking and some acquire a rosy blush, but colour is not always a good guide. To pick simply lift and gently twist; if they come off without resistance they are ready. Take great care not to bruise the fruit and if you intend to store them, lay them out in a single layer in a paper-lined tray. Place somewhere cool and dark.

Container growing

Pears are well suited to growing in large pots and containers, filled with loam-based John Innes No. 3 compost. Stand your tree – a self-fertile one if you don't have room for two – in a sunny position and water well during the growing season. When the tree is flowering you could move it into a greenhouse or conservatory to protect it from frost but you will have to pollinate the fruit with a small, soft paintbrush.

Feed your tree each week between April and September with a high potash feed to encourage fruit formation and ripening. Supplement this by adding some controlled-release fertiliser.

Calendar

● Plant during dormant season Oct–Mar.
● Buy 3-year-old, part fan-trained trees if you are impatient for a crop.
● Plant against a warm wall.

	JAN	FEB	MAR	APR	MAY	JUN	JUL	AUG	SEP	OCT	NOV	DEC
Planting time	■	■	■							■	■	■
Harvest time									■	■		

Plums are addictive. Plant a tree in your garden, wait for it to become heavily laden with ripe, juicy fruit, then try to resist eating them straight from the tree! Plums have the advantage of needing very little care. Just a well-sheltered, sunny spot and ideally a deep, moisture-retentive soil. When it comes to pruning, the message is, less is best!

Varieties

There is a wide variety of plums, including culinary (cooking), dessert (eating) and dual-purpose varieties, as well as the closely related damsons and gages. Some are relatively new and all have their own flavours and characteristics.

Of the desserts, the most popular plum for many years has been 'Victoria'. A very heavy cropping variety, it used to grow into a very large tree, so was not suitable for small gardens. However, dwarfing rootstocks such as St Julien A and Pixy have helped to make it, and other varieties, more manageable.

Growing tips

Planting
Trees should be planted during the dormant season (October to March) and are quite tolerant of poor growing conditions; however, to do well they prefer a sunny, sheltered spot

where neither cold winds nor frost will damage the blossom.

Although some varieties such as 'Victoria' and the cooking variety 'Czar' are self-fertile, many others are not and you will need to check with your supplier as to whether another tree will be necessary to ensure good pollination. Of course, self-fertile varieties can be used to pollinate others that fruit at the same time.

Dig in plenty of organic matter such as garden compost or manure prior to planting – the autumn before if possible – as this helps the soil to hold on to water during the dry summer months once it has rotted down well.

Make sure that the graft is well above soil level, using the water or soil mark on the trunk as a guide. Fans, cordons and other wall-trained forms will need to have horizontal support wires set up before planting at about 45cm/18in apart.

Growing on
Plum trees do not need pruning after planting in the winter. In fact any pruning – in the case of an established bush tree removing crossing, damaged or dead branches – should be done between April and June and kept to a minimum. For the pruning of cordons, see Apples (page 95). Pruning in the growing season, when the sap is rising, helps to keep silver leaf and bacterial canker at bay; both can be, although rarely are, fatal to the tree.

Wasps can be a problem when the plums are ripening, taking advantage of damage caused by pecking birds. Cover low-growing clusters of fruit with netting and hang wasp traps in the tree.

Fact file
- Botanically, plums are classed as drupes – each fruit contains a single seed.
- If late frosts are a problem in your garden, then look to gages, which are a little less prone to frost damage than plums.
- In years when crops are heavy, it may be necessary to support the branches to prevent them breaking under the weight.

- When picking, gently lift and twist the fruit, taking care not to bruise it.

In the kitchen

Late summer's colourful array of plums varies in sweetness and texture, but all have their place in the kitchen. Eat the sweet, large watery ones and cook with the smaller, firm, sour ones.

Preparation and cooking: Pick while slightly under ripe. Firm plums are easier to prepare and will ripen well in the warmth of the kitchen.

Plums are very versatile and have a distinctive flavour. Plum jam is delicious; the stoned fruit can be frozen for use in pies and pastries during the winter months. Small, firm plums are best for cooking and will reduce into a sharp sticky sauce that goes well with duck, venison and game. A plum glut is best resolved with a tasty batch of chutneys, jams and jellies.

Storage and freezing: The skin is edible but can be tart and tough. To remove, blanch in boiling water then plunge into cold; the skins should slip away easily. Freeze the fruit in one of three ways: whole, in sections in a sugar syrup, or as purée. In all cases, they are best stored either in freezer-proof containers or zipped freezer bags.

To freeze in syrup, wash and quarter the fruit, removing the stones. Make up the syrup by adding 1 cup of hot water to 1 cup of sugar, plus ½ tsp ascorbic acid to each litre of syrup. Dissolve the sugar and allow to cool before pouring over the fruit in a suitable container or freezer bag. Make sure the fruit is covered and that all the air is forced from the bag prior to sealing.

♥ High in vitamin A and potassium, plus useful amounts of vitamin C and folate (vitamin B9).

Container growing

Plums are not best suited for growing in pots, although they will survive and crop reasonably well. Growing in large containers does have the advantage of being able to move the trees out of the frost when flowering, but it is best to take the tree back outside once the flowers have set fruit. Plant in John Innes No. 3 potting compost.

It is also possible to buy trees trained as fans, pyramids, cordons and minarettes – varieties grown on a single main stem – which can be grown in any sheltered spot or against a wall or fence, even in a flower garden with limited space. Trained trees such as these are ideal for exposed gardens where the blooms may be damaged by frost or cold winds.

PLUM AND MARZIPAN TREATS

The baked plums and marzipan can also be cooked in a puff pastry base with a little sugar syrup to make a tart. Lay them on the pastry, marzipan-side up, instead of making them into parcels, then bake as below.

2 ripe dessert plums per person, halved and stoned
250g/9oz marzipan
Ground almonds for sprinkling

1 Preheat the oven to 200°C/400°F/gas 6/fan oven 180°C. Fill the stone cavities of the plums with the marzipan.
2 Close the plum halves back together and hold in place with foil or greaseproof paper parcels, the latter tied with string. Bake for 20 minutes to soften the plums, but remove if they begin to lose too much juice. Alternatively cook on the hob in a heavy-based pan.
3 Unwrap and sprinkle the ground almonds over each plum half.

Serve with: Crème fraîche, yoghurt or ice cream.

Calendar

- Plant trees Oct–Mar.
- Prune Apr–Jun.
- Cover flowers at night where possible when frosts are expected.
- Harvest Jul–Sep.

	JAN	FEB	MAR	APR	MAY	JUN	JUL	AUG	SEP	OCT	NOV	DEC
Planting time	■	■	■							■	■	■
Harvest time							■	■	■			

Raspberries

Apart from their great taste and easy-going nature which makes them simple to grow, rapsberries are heavy cropping and versatile in the kitchen. They love moisture and will grow well against a shady wall, but are not happy in a hot, sunny position unless given lots of water and a thick mulch. They do need plenty of space and strong supports.

Varieties

Raspberries are divided into two groups, those that fruit in the summer and those that fruit from August to October. By choosing plants from each group, it is possible to be picking over a number of months. For example, you could choose:

'Glen Moy': One of the earliest varieties for July.

'Glen Ample': Follows the above in July–August.

'Octavia': A great variety for mid July to late August.

'Allgold': Sweet and yellow-fruited. Crops mid August to mid October.

Growing tips

Planting

Since raspberry plants (canes) will crop for anything up to 15 years before they need replacing, make sure you prepare the soil well. Dig in plenty of well-rotted garden compost or manure to help the soil hold water and rake in some general fertiliser or pelleted chicken manure about a week prior to planting.

Fact file

- Raspberries have been grown for more than 400 years in the British Isles.
- The berries are not berries at all, but a cluster of individual 'drupelets', each with a seed inside – like a mini version of a plum. These form around a central core, which remains on the plant when the ripe fruit is picked.
- Raspberries are a member of the rose family (*Rosaceae*).

Traditionally, posts and wires are used to support the canes, but it is possible to grow them against a wall or fence using trellis or wires held taut with vine eyes. The wires should be 45cm/18in apart up the supporting wall, fence or posts and 5–7cm/2–3in away from the wall. Plant the canes 45cm/18in apart with 1.5m/5ft between the rows.

Growing on

Apply a layer of garden compost or manure (mulch) to the canes every March after feeding with a dressing of general fertiliser or pelleted chicken manure. Tie in the canes as they grow to prevent wind damage.

Raspberries fruit on canes produced in the previous season, while also growing the canes which will fruit next year, so train the fruiting canes one way and the new canes the other, or train the new canes directly upwards from the roots and the older fruiting canes along the wires to the left and right.

In the case of summer-fruiting varieties all the

In the kitchen

Best eaten when the fruits have a warm purple glow and are soft, succulent, sweet and musky.

Preparation and cooking: As they ripen, the fruit separate from their core leaving an inner cavity so preparation is easy. Simply pick and rinse just before use. Cluster berries such as these have thin papery skins that make them fragile and perishable. Handle carefully, and try spreading in thin layers rather than piling high and bruising.

Raspberries are extremely versatile and are used in jams, preserves and jellies. They are also delicious made into tasty tarts, crumbles (good for using up frozen raspberries) and summer puddings. Their intense flavour and sweetness also lends itself well to game and rich meats.

Storage and freezing: Raspberries freeze surprisingly well: open freeze them by spreading the berries in a single layer on a baking tray and when frozen, transfer them into bags, driving out any excess air before returning to the freezer. To defrost, spread them out individually.

♥ *Rich in vitamin C, calcium, iron and potassium and useful amounts of B vitamins. A single cupful has a third of our recommended daily amount of fibre.*

fruited wood is cut down to ground level in the autumn, leaving the young canes intact to fruit next year. Autumn fruiters are pruned in late winter, with all the shoots being cut down to ground level. They do not need permanent supports and can simply be kept neat by tying around with string to poles.

RASPBERRY AND BRANDY TIRAMISU

Serves 2–3

120ml/4fl oz sweetened cold black coffee
2 tbsp brandy or Grand Marnier
150g/5oz raspberries
120ml/4fl oz whipping cream
1 tsp sugar
100g/4oz mascarpone cheese
½ tsp vanilla extract
8 sponge fingers
1 tbsp grated plain chocolate

1 Mix the coffee, brandy and fruit together and leave to stand for 30 minutes.
2 Whip the cream and sugar together until the mixture forms soft peaks.
3 Mix the mascarpone, a quarter of the coffee mixture and the vanilla together before gently folding in the cream.
4 Lay the sponge fingers in the bottom of a deep dish and pour the remaining coffee mixture over the top before spooning over the cream and mascarpone mixture.
5 Sprinkle the grated chocolate over the top and refrigerate for 2 hours before serving.

Container growing

Raspberries are not ideal plants for pots. However, if you just want the experience of growing your own raspberries, you could grow a few canes in a very large pot or tub – at least 60cm/2ft in diameter. Fill with John Innes No. 3 compost and after planting cover the surface with a bark mulch. Place it in a partly shaded spot and keep well watered. Tie some string around the canes for support.

Calendar

● Best planted or moved when dormant during the winter when the canes have no leaves.
● By choosing the right varieties you can pick raspberries Jul–Oct.

	JAN	FEB	MAR	APR	MAY	JUN	JUL	AUG	SEP	OCT	NOV	DEC
Planting time	■	■	■								■	■
Harvest time							■	■	■	■		

Rhubarb

Rhubarb is probably the easiest of all fruit and vegetable crops to grow in your garden or allotment, as it can simply be left to produce a harvest of colourful leaf stalks with little attention. It's ideal for everyone, even complete beginners. However, for the best thick and tasty stalks, some care is needed during the season.

Varieties

'Glaskin's Perpetual': Often listed in seed catalogues, but rhubarb grown from seed can be rather variable. Tasty deep red stems.
'Timperley Early': A good one for forcing, producing pale pink stems.
'Victoria': A late variety with red stems in late spring.

Growing tips

Planting
It is possible to grow rhubarb from seed, but the best plants are of named varieties grown by dividing existing crowns. Plant rhubarb from October to February in an open, sunny site in soil that has been given plenty of well-rotted garden compost or manure.

Growing on
Spread a thick layer of organic matter around the plants every winter and water well in the summer. Feed once harvesting ceases to boost plants for the next season. Although it's not essential, plants remain more vigorous if you dig them up and divide them every three years in the winter when they are dormant, making sure that each of your new plants has at least one bud and some healthy roots.

Left to its own devices, rhubarb should crop from March until July, when harvesting stops to allow the plant time to recover. It is possible, however, to harvest a little earlier by forcing. This merely involves popping an upturned bucket, dustbin or rhubarb forcer over the plant in January, thus excluding light and protecting the crowns to encourage earlier stalks (see picture below).

Rhubarb is not suitable for growing in containers.

Fact file
● Officially rhubarb is classed as a vegetable because the part of the plant that we eat is not a seed-producing fruit but a leaf stalk.
● Rhubarb leaves are poisonous and should never be eaten. However, they can be composted since by the time the leaves have broken down in the heat, the toxins will have disappeared.

Calendar
● Sow seeds Mar–Apr and grow in pots for their first year.
● Harvest newly planted crowns in second season until end Jul.
● Water crowns well in summer and mulch with organic matter.

	JAN	FEB	MAR	APR	MAY	JUN	JUL	AUG	SEP	OCT	NOV	DEC
Sowing/ planting time	■	■	■	■						■	■	■
Harvest time		■	■	■	■	■	■					

Strawberries

Growing tips

Sowing and planting

Strawberries can be grown easily from seed, which will produce plants very quickly when sown in the spring to give a good crop in their first year. However, it is more usual to buy strawberries as ready-grown plants called runners. It is important to buy them from a reliable source to ensure virus-free stock.

If planting in the garden, make sure that your

Strawberries are just as happy in a strawberry pot on the patio or in a hanging basket as they are in the soil and once you have tasted a home-grown strawberry you will never want to buy them from a supermarket again. You'll simply be able to pick and eat the fruit. Choose the right varieties and you can be picking from June to mid October.

Varieties

There are numerous summer and perpetual strawberries available and it is a good idea to check catalogues supplied by fruit specialists before buying. Strawberries fall into three main types:

SUMMER FRUITING

Early fruiting varieties crop from mid June to early July, mid-season varieties a week later. Late fruiting types begin to crop in July.

PERPETUAL VARIETIES

These produce a small amount of fruit in summer with the bulk from mid August to mid October.

ALPINE STRAWBERRIES

Grown from seeds, alpines are sold by most seed companies. The plants are decorative and ideal for pots or as edging for the flower border, although keep them under control as they can spread everywhere.

Fact file

- For early fruit, cover some plants with cloches or several layers of horticultural fleece at night from early May.
- Plants in pots or growbags can be moved into a frost-free greenhouse, ventilated during the day to allow pollinating insects to reach the blooms.
- Growbags offer a simple way to grow your plants. Plant 6–8 runners in each bag and feed occasionally with a high potash tomato food.

STRAWBERRIES WITH BALSAMIC CONDIMENT AND BLACK PEPPER

Serves 3–4

450g/1lb strawberries, hulled
25g/1oz caster sugar
1 tsp balsamic condiment
freshly ground black pepper
vanilla ice cream to serve (optional)

1 Place the strawberries in a ceramic bowl with the sugar and vinegar. Mix thoroughly and chill.
2 Before serving, sprinkle generously with black pepper. Add vanilla ice cream if you wish.

strawberries are in an area that will not become waterlogged in winter. Simply plant into weed-free soil, into which you have dug well-rotted manure or garden compost the previous autumn. As your strawberries will remain in the same spot for three years or more, you can prevent weeds from building up, by planting them through a mulch of polythene or ground-cover fabric.

In the kitchen

You will be lucky if any of your strawberries reach the kitchen, as the whole family will enjoy picking and eating them straight from the plant. Pick regularly and if intending to keep them for a few days, don't remove the stalk.

Preparation and cooking: Ripen strawberries on the plant, and eat them on the day of picking. As a change from sugar and cream, enhance their sweetness with freshly ground black pepper and/or a drizzle of balsamic vinegar (try the recipe opposite). Strawberry jam and preserves (in which the fruit is kept whole) have always been favourites and are relatively easy to make. They are also a great way to preserve fruit if you have a glut. However, they are poor in pectin, so use a preserving sugar with added pectin to ensure a good set. Strawberries also make wonderful sorbets, ice creams, sauces, tarts – the list is never ending.

Storage and freezing: Soft, juicy strawberries do not keep well. Even careful cold storage will not prevent fruit turning mushy and bruised. They will keep in the fridge if picked just ripe, but it is important to eat them within a few days.

Strawberries can be frozen although they lose their firmness when thawed; wash and dry each fruit, discarding (or eating) any damaged specimens. Drop small batches into a freezer bag and force out as much of the air as possible. Alternatively freeze the pulped fruit.
♥ *High in vitamin C and antioxidants.*

Calendar

● Buy freshly dug strawberry plants Oct–Nov, or Mar–July using plants that have been held in a cold store.
● The latter often fruits in as little as 60 days after planting.

	JAN	FEB	MAR	APR	MAY	JUN	JUL	AUG	SEP	OCT	NOV	DEC
Planting time			■	■	■	■		■		■	■	
Harvest time						■	■	■	■			

Plant strawberries with the crown (growing point) just above soil level; it will put out runners on which new plantlets will grow.

Growing on

Feed the plants in spring with sulphate of potash at the rate of 15g per sqm/½oz per sq yd to give them a boost in preparation for fruiting. Avoid nitrogen feeds as these encourage lots of leafy growth at the expense of berries.

During the winter remove all the old growth, before plants begin to send up new leaves, and remove runners, which tend to sap the plants' energy. If your plants are young and healthy with no signs of virus, some of the best-rooted runners can be planted in pots or in rows on the plot to make new plants for fruiting next year.

STRAWBERRY GRANITA

Serves 4–6

Granita is a refreshing, fat-free alternative to ice cream on a hot, sunny day and is served as slightly slushy ice.

175g/6oz brown sugar
600ml/1pt strawberry purée (fresh or frozen fruit)
150ml/¼pt white or redcurrant juice, or orange juice
150ml/¼pt water
juice of 1 lemon
sprig of mint to garnish (optional)

1 Dissolve the brown sugar in the strawberry purée (the sugar can be whizzed together with the fruit in the blender when making the purée). Then whisk in the remaining ingredients.
2 Freeze the mixture in a large, shallow bowl for 2 hours before removing from the freezer and stirring with a fork. Replace for another hour and stir it again.
3 Allow the granita to thaw a little prior to serving, forking it through if necessary (it will remain 'soft' for a few hours in the fridge). Garnish with mint, if you wish.

Container growing

Strawberries are ideal for growing in containers, plant in any fresh multi-purpose compost – although a John Innes type is best; make sure that the growing point stays just above the level of the compost. You can buy special strawberry pots with holes in the side so you can plant one runner in each. Alternatively plant three into the top of a hanging basket, with more around the edge, or four or five in a growbag. You can also plant in rows in the garden, allowing about 30cm/12in between each plant. Choose a sunny spot to grow your plants.

Useful terms

Annual: A plant that lasts a single season.

Antioxidants: Molecules that help prevent the breakdown of chemicals, thus reducing the number of potentially harmful free radicals in the body. Free radicals may cause damage to the cells in the body, leading to the formation of cancers.

Base dressing: An application of organic matter or fertiliser, applied to the soil prior to planting or sowing.

Beta carotene: Plant pigment that gives orange carrots their distinctive colour. Leads to development of vitamin A, which protects against cancer and heart disease.

Biennial: A plant with a two-year life cycle.

Blanch: The practice of excluding light to produce sweeter tasting leaves and stems, e.g. endive (see page 35). To immerse in boiling water to soften or remove skins perhaps in preparation for freezing.

Bolt: To flower and produce seed prematurely.

Brassica: A member of the cabbage family (*Brassicaceae*).

Broadcast: To scatter granular substances such as seeds, fertiliser or pesticide evenly over an area of ground.

Capping: A crust forming on the surface of soil damaged by compaction, watering or rainfall.

Cell tray (or module): Containers used for propagating and growing young plants in single units for easy transplanting.

Chitting: Pre-germination of seeds or seed potatoes prior to sowing.

Cloche: A small portable cover used to protect crops outdoors from frost.

Cold frame: A small, unheated covered structure used to harden off young seedlings or grow tender crops.

Compost: Decomposed organic waste from the garden or kitchen used as a mulch or soil conditioner. Also a potting or seed-sowing medium.

Crown: The central base of a plant from which shoots and roots grow.

Cultivar: A new plant variant produced as the result of intentionally crossing two plants.

Damp down: To wet the floors and benches in a greenhouse or polytunnel in order to increase humidity and lower high temperatures.

Division: Splitting a clump into smaller portions.

Dormancy: Period when a plant stops growing during the winter months.

Earth up: To pull soil up around the base of a plant for support, to deter frost or to cover a plant for the purpose of blanching; to prevent potatoes from turning green.

Enzymes: Proteins that speed up reactions and drive the living process in the body.

Essential oil: A volatile oil contained in many plants such as rosemary and basil.

Evergreen: Plants that keep their leaves all year.

F1 hybrid: Plants obtained by crossing two selected pure-breeding parents to produce uniform, heavy cropping offspring.

Fertiliser: A material applied to the soil or plants to provide nutrition.

Fleece: Fine mesh insulating cover used to protect crops from cold and pests.

Folate: A naturally occuring B vitamin (B9) often found in fruit and vegetables. Folic acid is the synthetic form of folate.

Forking (or fanging): Damage to a root vegetable, such as carrot, in the development stage causing it to grow a fork-like 'leg'.

Friable: A soil with a crumbly, workable texture, capable of forming a tilth, such as in a seedbed.

Frost pockets: Areas where cold air collects, often at the base of slopes.

Fungicide: Chemical used to control fungal diseases.

Germination: The process of growth from dormant seed to seedling.

Graft: Join between the root and fruiting wood – the fruiting part is joined to the roots from another tree to control its growth; the knobble on the stem marking this point must be well above soil level after planting.

Green manure: A fast-growing crop grown for digging into the soil, to improve its structure and nutrient levels.

Growbag: A bag of compost sold for use as a growing medium for producing salad crops and herbs.

Half hardy: Plants that grow in low temperatures but will not withstand frost.

Harden off: To accustom plants to lower temperatures prior to planting outside.

Hardy: Plants that can tolerate frost without protection.

Haulm: The top growth of plants such as potatoes.

Heart up: The stage at which leafy vegetables swell to form a central heart.

Heavy soil: A soil, such as a clay, which holds a lot of water and becomes hard when dry.

Herbaceous: Non-woody plants that die down at the end of the season, coming up again the next year – e.g. asparagus (see page 11).

Herbicide: A chemical used to kill weeds.

Humus: The organic decayed remains of plant material in soils that binds the particles together.

Hybrid: A plant resulting from the breeding of two distinct species or genera.

Infusion: A tea made by steeping leaves in boiling water.

Inorganic: Term used to describe fertilisers made from naturally occurring minerals, or artificial fertilisers.

Insecticide: Chemical used to kill insect pests.

John Innes compost: Loam-based growing medium made to a standard recipe.

Leaching: The washing out, and loss of, soluble nutrients from topsoil.

Leaf: A plant organ containing the green pigment (chlorophyll) essential for photosynthesis.

Leaf mould: A peat-like material, which is the result of decaying leaves.

Legume: The pea and bean family.

Lime: Calcium used to raise the pH (alkalinity) of the soil.

Loam: Fertile soil of medium texture.

Maincrop: The biggest crop produced throughout the growing season.

Minarettes: Small varieties of fruit tree grown on a single main stem, with short fruiting side spurs, suitable for containers.

Minerals: Natural compounds used in the body to help many processes and often associated with enzymes.

Mulch: A layer of material applied to the ground to control weeds, conserve moisture and protect the soil.

Neutral: Soil or compost with a pH value of seven, which is neither acid nor alkaline.

Nutrients: Minerals essential for plant growth.

Organic: Term used to describe substances that are derived from natural sources, e.g. plant waste. Also used to describe gardening without the use of chemicals.

Pan: A layer of compacted soil that prevents the movement of water and oxygen, impeding root development and drainage.

Perennial: A plant that lives for three or more years.

Perlite and vermiculite: Forms of expanded volcanic rock used in propagation and to improve drainage in potting composts.

pH: A measure of acidity or alkalinity in the soil or compost based on a scale of 0 to 14. A pH below seven is acid and above, alkaline.

Pinch out: To remove the growing tip of a plant to encourage branching.

Pot on: To move a plant into a larger pot as the roots develop and grow too big for the pot.

Potassium: A mineral essential for our cells to ensure that they function correctly.

Prick out: To transfer seedlings, from a seedbed or tray, with the purpose of giving them room to grow.

Propagation: The process of increasing plant stocks by seed or vegetative means (cuttings or division).

Radicle: The root of a seedling.

Rhizome: A fleshy underground stem that acts as a storage organ.

Root: The part of the plant that absorbs water and nutrients and anchors the plant.

Root crops: Vegetables grown for their edible roots.

Runner: A trailing shoot that roots where it touches the ground, e.g. strawberry (see page 122).

Seed: A dormant embryo, capable of forming a plant.

Seed leaves or cotyledons: The first leaf or leaves produced by a seed following germination.

Seedbed: A small area of dug and raked soil.

Seedling: A young plant grown from seed.

Sets: Small onions or shallots used for planting.

Shoot: A branch or stem.

Side shoot: A branch or stem growing from the main stem.

Slit trench: A trench made by inserting the blade of a spade into the soil and moving it back and forth.

Species: A group of closely related plants with similar characteristics.

Stamen: The male pollen-producing part of the plant.

Stem: The main shoot of a plant, from which side shoots appear.

Stigma: The part of a pistil (the female organs of a flower) that receives pollen.

Subsoil: Layers of less fertile soil immediately below the topsoil, often lighter in colour.

Sucker: A stem originating below soil level, usually from the plant's roots or underground stem, as in raspberries.

Systemic or translocated: A term used to describe a chemical that is absorbed by a plant at one point and then circulated by the sap.

Tap root: The main anchoring root of a plant, usually growing straight down into the soil. Often a storage organ, e.g. carrot (see page 26).

Tender: Plants with little or no tolerance of frost.

Thinning: The uprooting of seedlings to improve the quality of those that remain. Also the removal of fruit or shoots to prevent overcrowding.

Tilth: The surface layer of soil produced by cultivation.

Top dressing: The application of fertilisers or bulky organic material to the soil surface or compost in a pot.

Topsoil: The upper, most fertile layer of soil.

Transpiration: The evaporation of moisture from plant leaves and stems via pores called stomata.

Transplant: To move a plant from one growing position to another.

Tuber: A modified underground stem used to store moisture and nutrients, e.g. potato (see page 59).

Variety: A botanical classification used to describe a naturally occurring plant variant (see also cultivar).

Vegetative: Parts of a plant that are capable of growth.

Vitamins: Nutrients required by the body, essential for metabolism (the chemical reactions that take place in living cells to allow them, and therefore our bodies, to function). They are separate from the many minerals that are also essential to keep us healthy.

Weathering: The effect of rain and frost on the soil.

Wind rock: Destabilisation of plant roots by the wind, especially after planting.

Index

apples 94–6
apricots 97
artichokes 10
asparagus 11–2
aubergines 13

baked blackberry cheesecake 100
barbecued sweetcorn with chilli and
    lime butter 73
basil 80
    herby cheese tomatoes 76
bay 81
beetroot 14–5
blackberries 98–100
blackcurrants 105–6
blue cheese and crunch dressing 67
blueberries 101–2
    apple and blueberry pie 96
borders, as vegetable plots 8
broad beans 16–7
broccoli 18–9
Brussels sprouts 20–1
bubble and squeak 61

cabbages 22–3
carrots 26–7
cauliflowers 24–5
celeriac 28
celery 29
cheese
    blue cheese and crunch dressing 67
    cheese-baked leeks 46
    cheesy tomato tartlets 77
    crunchy baked cauliflower 25
    herby cheese tomatoes 76
    roasted pumpkin and cheese parcels 71
cheesecakes
    baked blackberry cheesecake 100
    cheesecake-style grape dessert 112
cheesy tomato tartlets 77
cherries 103–4
chicory 30
    endive and chicory salad 36
chilli
    barbecued sweetcorn with chilli and
        lime butter 73
    chilli hot potatoes 61
    chilli prawn salad 58
    chilli-spiced beans 38
Chinese pork in lettuce parcels 48
chives 82
chutney, spicy gooseberry 110
cinnamon spiced parsnips 54
container growing 8

coriander 83
    carrot and coriander soup 27
courgettes 31–2
crab apples 94
cucumbers 33–4
currants 105–6

dill 84

endive 35–6

fennel 85
figs 107–8
flognarde with peaches 114
French beans 37–8
    tarragon and three-bean salad 64
fruity parsnips 54

garlic 39–40
    courgette and slow-roasted garlic soup 32
gazpacho 40
globe artichokes 10
gooseberries 109–10
granita, strawberry 124
grapes 111–2

herby cheese tomatoes 76

kale 41–2
kohlrabi 43

lawns, new plots from 7–8
leeks 44–6
lettuces 47–8

marjoram 86
marrows 31–2
mint 87
    herby cheese tomatoes 76
muffins, beetroot 15

nectarines 113–4
neglected plots 7

onions 49–51

parsley 88
    herby cheese tomatoes 76
parsnips 52–4
peaches 113–4
pears 115–6
peas 55–6
peppers 57–8

pies
  apple and blueberry pie 96
  cabbage pie 23
planting 8
plums 117–8
poached pears, traditional 116
potatoes 59–61
preparation 7–8
pumpkins 69–71

radishes 62
raspberries 119–20
redcurrants 105–6
rhubarb 121
roasted pumpkin and cheese parcels 71
rosemary 89
runner beans 63–4

sage 90
salads
  blue cheese and crunch dressing 67
  chilli prawn salad 58
  endive and chicory salad 36
  salad leaves 65–7
  savory bean salad 17
  tarragon and three-bean salad 64
  warm salad of baby leeks 45
sandwiches, cucumber with cream cheese and
  black pepper 34
sauce, apple 96
savory bean salad 17
seeds, sowing 8
sesame kale 42
shallots 49–51
soups
  broccoli and Stilton soup 19
  carrot and coriander soup 27
  courgette and slow-roasted garlic soup 32
  gazpacho 40

spicy gooseberry chutney 110
spicy squash 71
spinach 68
  spinach peas 56
sprouts 20–1
squashes 69–71
strawberries 122–4
stuffed onions 51
summer squash 69–71
sweet and nutty sprouts 21
sweet bay 81
sweetcorn 72–3
Swiss chard 74

tarragon 91
  tarragon and three-bean salad 64
tarts
  asparagus tart 12
  cheesy tomato tartlets 77
  fig tarte tatin 108
  onion upside-down tart 51
thyme 92
tiramisu
  cherry tiramisu 104
  raspberry and brandy tiramisu 120
tomatoes 75–7
traditional poached pears 116
turf, removing 7
turnips 78

vinegar, blackberry 99

warm salad of baby leeks 45
warming winter pudding 106
weeds, dealing with 7–8
whitecurrants 105–6
winter squash 69–71